Student Book

American Headway 2

John and Liz Soars

OXFORD
UNIVERSITY PRESS

Oxford University Press
198 Madison Avenue
New York, NY 10016 USA

Great Clarendon Street
Oxford OX2 6DP England

Oxford New York

Auckland Cape Town Dar es Salaam Hong Kong Karachi
Kuala Lumpur Madrid Melbourne Mexico City Nairobi
New Delhi Shanghai Taipei Toronto

With offices in

Argentina Austria Brazil Chile Czech Republic France Greece
Guatemala Hungary Italy Japan South Korea Poland Portugal
Singapore Switzerland Thailand Turkey Ukraine Vietnam

OXFORD is a trademark of Oxford University Press.

Copyright © 2001 Oxford University Press

Library of Congress Cataloging-in-Publication Data

Soars, John
American headway. Student book 2 / John and Liz Soars.
    p. cm.
ISBN-13: 978-0-19-435379-3
ISBN-10: 0-19-435379-6
    1. English language—Textbooks for foreign speakers. 2. English
language—United States—Problems, exercises, etc. 3. Americanisms—
Problems, exercises, etc. I. Soars, Liz. II. Title.
PE 1128 .S5935 2001
428.2'4—dc21   200132196

American Headway Student Book 2:
Editorial Manager: Shelagh Speers
Managing Editor: Jeff Krum
Editor: Pat O'Neill
Editorial Assistant: Alicia Dunn
Art Director: Lynn Luchetti
Designer: Shelley Himmelstein
Art Buyer/Picture Researcher: Laura Nash
Production Manager: Shanta Persaud
Production Coordinator: Eve Wong

Printing (last digit): 10 9 8

Printed in China.

Acknowledgments

Cover concept: Rowie Christopher
Cover design: Rowie Christopher and Silver Editions

Illustrations by Wesley Bates; Frank Bolle/American Artists Rep. Inc.; Carlos
Castellanos; Rowie Christopher; Paul Dickenson; Hal Just; Tim Kahane; Ian
Kellas; Beverly Levy; Gone Loco, Debut Art; J. F. Martin; Fanny Mellet Berry;
Oxford University Press (UK) TechGraphics; Pierre Paul Pariseau; Andy Parker;
Steve Pica; Rodica Prato; Carol Strebel; Harry Venning; Azélie Williams

Handwriting and realia by Rae Grant, Susumu Kawabe

Location and studio photography by Gareth Boden, Dennis Kitchen, Mark
Mason, Alexandre Militão, Laura Nash, Stephen Ogilvy

*The publishers would like to thank the following for their permission to reproduce
photographs:* S. Adams/Telegraph Colour Library, L. Adamski Peek/Getty One
Stone, Advertising Archives, M. Agliolo/Science Photo Library, AKG London,
Alaska Stock, F. Alison/Getty One Stone, The Ancient Art & Architecture
Collection, The Anthony Blake Photo Library, AP, B. Apicella/Photofusion,
D. Armand/Getty One Stone, Guy Aroch/Corbis Outline, The Art Archive,
B. Backman/Colorific!, Dave Bartruff/Corbis, C. Bernson/Colorific!, I. Berry/
Magnum Photos, Bettmann/Corbis, Ed Bock/Corbis Stock Market, J. & C.
Bord/Fortean Picture Library, G. Buntrock/The Anthony Blake Photo Library,
Michele Burgess/Corbis Stock Market, H. Camille/Getty One Stone,

J. Carnemolla/Australian Picture Library, Terry Cemm/Anthony Coleman,
R. Chapple/Telegraph Colour Library, Jason Childs/FPG, Columbia/*Close
Encounters of the Third Kind*/Pictorial Press, Comstock, Corbis, Corbis Stock
Market, R.E. Daemrich/Getty One Stone, J. Danielsky/Telegraph Colour Library,
D. Day/Getty One Stone, F. Delva/Telegraph Colour Library, D. Dickinson/Int'l
Stock/Robert Harding Picture Library, George B. Diebold/The Stock Market,
Digital Vision, D. Ducros/Science Photo Library, Duomo/Corbis, R. During/
Getty One Stone, L. Dutton/Getty One Stone, B. Edmaier/Science Photo
Library, C. Ehlers/Getty One Stone, R. Elliot/Getty One Stone, Evans/Hulton
Getty, T. Fincher/Photographers International, G. Fonluft/Frank Spooner
Pictures, K. Fisher/Getty One Stone, FPG, J.P. Fruchet/Telegraph Colour Library,
R. Gage/Telegraph Colour Library, Getty News Services/MGM, Michael
Goldman/FPG, T. Graham/Colorific!, Lauren Greenfield, L. Greenfield/Corbis
Sygma, Sally & Richard Greenhill, D. Ham/Getty One Stone, John Henley/The
Stock Market, R. Holmes/Corbis, Hulton Getty, M. Hutson/Redferns, Image
Bank, Images Colour Library, F. Jalain/Robert Harding Picture Library, David
James 1998 TM & Dreamworks LLC Paramount Pictures Amblin Entertainment.
All Rights Reserved/*Saving Private Ryan*/The Kobal Collection, J. Tove Johansson/
Colorific!, Jordan/Frank Spooner Pictures, W. Kaehler/Getty One Stone, Michael
Keller/Corbis Stock Market, KOBAL/Universal © 1982, P. Langone/Int'l
Stock/Robert Harding Picture Library, R. La Salle/Getty One Stone, P. Lay/The
Telegraph, Lightscapes Inc./The Stock Market, Lucasfilm/Paramount '81/*Raiders
of the Lost Ark*/The Kobal Collection, D. Madison/Getty One Stone, R. Mancini/
The Image Bank, McDonald's, Ryan McVay/PhotoDisc, Doug Menuez/PhotoDisc,
S. Miller/Telegraph Colour Library, D. Modricker/COR/Corbis, L. Monneret/
Getty One Stone, M. Mutor/Agencja Gazeta, Office of Information for Puerto
Rico/Hulton Getty, I. O'Leary/Getty One Stone, C. Osborne/Corbis, Oxford
University Press/Oxford Picture Library, Gregory Pace/Corbis/Sygma, A.
Pasieka/Science Photo Library, PBJ Pictures/Getty One Stone, H. Pfeiffer/Getty
One Stone, PhotoDisc, Picture Press/Corbis, P. Plailly/Science Photo Library,
Colin Raw/Stone, Reiss/Hulton Getty, Reuters NewMedia Inc./Corbis, N.
Reynard/Frank Spooner Pictures, Robert Harding Picture Library, Martin
Rogers/Stone, Rohan/Getty One Stone, M. Romanelli/The Image Bank,
K. Ross/Telegraph Colour Library, G.A. Rossi/The Image Bank, Royal Asiatic
Society/The Bridgeman Art Library, P. Scholey/Telegraph Colour Library,
H. Schwarzbach/Still Pictures, Ariel Skelly/Corbis Stock Market, Solo
Syndication Ltd., Stone, Strauss/Curtis/Corbis Stock Market, Superstock,
A. Sydenham/The Anthony Blake Photo Library, B. Thomas/Getty One Stone,
Henry Thomas/KOBAL Universal © 1982, Rico Torres/KOBAL Dimension
© 1995, Dan Tremain/PhotoDisc, J. van Hasselt/Corbis Sygma, TM & © 1993
Universal City Studios and Amblin Entertainment. All Rights Reserved/*Schindler's
List*/The Kobal Collection, UPI/*Jurassic Park*/Pictorial Press, Warner Bros./The
Kobal Collection, Wartenberg/Picture Press/Corbis, White Castle, Larry
Williams/Corbis Stock Market, D. Willis/Stock Shot, J. Woodcock/Bubbles
Photo Library, Jeff Zaruba/The Stock Market, Zefa/The Stock Market
Special thanks to Ziggy Himmelstein, the Brooklyn Conservatory of Music

The publishers would also like to thank the following for their help:
p. 18 "The Burglar's Friend" *The Daily Mail* February 5, 1996, © *The Daily
    Mail*/Solo Syndication. Used by permission.
p. 23 *The Man with the Golden Gun* by Ian Fleming © Glidrose Publications.
    Used by permission.
p. 31 "The Best Shopping Street in the World" by Anne Applebaum, *London
    Evening Standard* October 27, 1998, © *London Evening Standard*/Solo
    Syndication. Used by permission.
p. 40 "You've Got a Friend" Words and music by Carole King © 1971
    COLGEMS-EMI MUSIC INC. All Rights Reserved. International Copyright
    Secured. Used by Permission.
p. 47 "The Most Generous Man in the World" by Tony Burton, *Mail Weekend
    Magazine* December 31, 1994, © *Mail Weekend Magazine*/Solo Syndication.
    Used by permission.
p. 71 "One Day All this Will Be Offices" by Jonathon Glancey, *The Guardian*
    July 11, 1998, © *The Guardian*. Used by permission.
p. 74 "All Alone with My Rocky Horrors" by Paul Lay, *The Telegraph* October 3,
    1998. Reproduced by permission of Paul Lay.
p. 79 From INTO THE WILD by Jon Krakauer, copyright © 1996 by Jon
    Krakauer. Used by permission of Villiard Books, a division of Random
    House, Inc.
p. 86 *Seeds of Change* by Henry Hobhouse. Cover reproduced by permission of
    Macmillan Publishing Co., UK.
p. 102 "Lively Tom, 69, Skates on for Tesco" *The Daily Mail* February 18, 1999
    © *The Daily Mail*/Solo Syndication. Used by permission.
p. 110 "The tale of two silent brothers." From Oxford Bookworms: *Stories From
    the Five Towns*. Reproduced by permission of Jennifer Bassett.
p. 112 "Talk to Me" by Bruce Springsteen. Copyright © 1978 by Bruce
    Springsteen (ASCAP). Reprinted by permission.

Contents

SCOPE AND SEQUENCE

1 Getting to know you

Tenses · Questions · Using a bilingual dictionary · Social expressions 1

STARTER

1 Match the questions and answers.

Where were you born?	A year ago.
What do you do?	Three times a week.
Are you married?	In Thailand.
Why are you studying English?	Because I need it for my job.
When did you start learning English?	I'm a teacher.
How often do you have English classes?	No, I'm single.

2 Ask and answer the questions with a partner.

TWO STUDENTS
Tenses and questions

1 **T 1.1** Read and listen to Mauricio. Then complete the text using the verbs in the box.

'm enjoying	'm going to work	live	started
'm studying	come	can speak	went

My name's **Mauricio Nesta.** I (1) _come_ from Brasilia, the capital of Brazil. I'm a student at the University of Brasilia. I (2) _____ modern languages—English and French. I also know a little Spanish, so I (3) _____ four languages.
I (4) _____ the program a lot, but it's really hard work. I (5) _____ college three years ago.

I (6) _____ at home with my parents and my sister. My brother (7) _____ to work in the United States last year.

After I graduate, I (8) _____ as a translator. I hope so, anyway.

2 Complete the questions about Carly.

1. _Where does she_ come from?
    _____

2. _____ live?
    _____

3. _____ live with?
    _____

4. What _____ studying?
    _____

5. _____ enjoying the program?
    _____

6. How many _____ speak?
    _____

7. _____ did her program start?
    _____

8. What _____ after she graduates?
    _____

T 1.2 Listen to Carly, and write the answers to the questions above.

3 Carly is also a student. Read her answers, then complete the questions.

1. "What _university do you go_ to?"
    "I don't go to a university. I study at home."

2. "_____ a job?"
    "Yes, I do. A part-time job."

3. "What _____ right now?"
    "I'm reading about Italian art."

4. "_____ to the United States?"
    "Fifteen years ago."

5. "_____ name?"
    "Dave."

6. "_____?"
    "He's an architect."

Carly Robson

GRAMMAR SPOT

1   Find examples of present, past, and future tenses in Exercises 1 and 2 above.

2   Which tenses are the two verb forms in these sentences? What is the difference between them?
     He lives with his parents.
     She's living with a Canadian family for a month.

3   Match the question words and answers.

What ... ?	Because I wanted to.
Who ... ?	Last night.
Where ... ?	$5.00.
When ... ?	A sandwich.
Why ... ?	By bus.
How many ... ?	In Miami.
How much ... ?	Jack.
How ... ?	The black one.
Whose ... ?	It's mine.
Which ... ?	Four.

▶▶ **Grammar Reference 1.1 and 1.2 p. 139**

PRACTICE

Talking about you

1 Ask and answer questions with a partner.

- Where ... live?
- ... have any brothers or sisters?
- What ... like doing on weekends?
- Where ... go for your last vacation?

Make more questions. Use some of the question words in the Grammar Spot on page 3. Ask your teacher some of the questions.

2 In groups, ask and answer the questions.

- Do you like listening to music?
- What kind of music do you like?
- What are you wearing?
- What is your teacher wearing?
- What did you do last night?
- What are you doing tonight?

3 Write a paragraph about you. Use the text about Mauricio on page 2 to help you.

Getting information

4 Work with a partner.

You each have different information about Judy Dandridge, a mail carrier. Ask and answer questions.

Student A Go to page 114.
Student B Go to page 116.

Check it

5 Choose the correct verb form.
1. Maria *comes* / *is coming* from Chile.
2. She *speaks* / *is speaking* Spanish and English.
3. Today Tom *wears* / *is wearing* jeans and a T-shirt.
4. *Are you liking* / *Do you like* black coffee?
5. Last year she *went* / *goes* on vacation to Florida.
6. Next year she *studies* / *is going to study* at a university in California.

VOCABULARY
Using a bilingual dictionary

1 Look at this extract from the *Oxford Portuguese Minidictionary*.

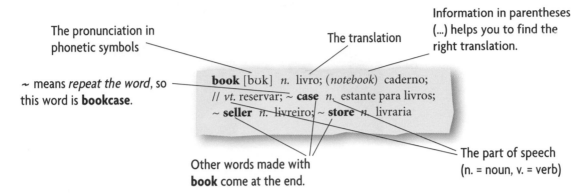

The pronunciation in phonetic symbols

The translation

Information in parentheses (...) helps you to find the right translation.

~ means *repeat the word*, so this word is **bookcase**.

book [bʊk] *n.* livro; (*notebook*) caderno; // *vt.* reservar; ~ **case** *n.* estante para livros; ~ **seller** *n.* livreiro; ~ **store** *n.* livraria

Other words made with **book** come at the end.

The part of speech (n. = noun, v. = verb)

2 What parts of speech are these words? Write *noun*, *verb*, *adjective*, *adverb*, *preposition*, or *past tense verb*.

bread	_noun_	beautiful	_____	on	_____
funny	_____	in	_____	came	_____
write	_____	never	_____	eat	_____
quickly	_____	went	_____	letter	_____

3 These words have more than one meaning. Write two sentences that show different meanings. Use a dictionary.

	Sentence 1	Sentence 2
1. book	I'm reading a good book.	I booked a room at a hotel.
2. kind		
3. can		
4. mean		
5. light		
6. play		
7. train		
8. ring		

T 1.3 Listen to some sample answers.

4 What are the everyday objects in the pictures? Look around the room you are in. Find five things you don't know the words for in English. Look them up in a dictionary.

READING
Communication

1 How many different ways can people communicate?

2 Work with a partner. You will get some ideas to communicate, but you can't use words. Mime the ideas.

Student A Go to page 118.
Student B Go to page 120.

3 Read the text on page 7 quickly and match the correct heading to each paragraph.

A **HISTORY** OF COMMUNICATION

HOW WE COMMUNICATE

COMMUNICATION **TODAY**

DIFFERENCES BETWEEN **PEOPLE** AND **ANIMALS**

4 Read the text again and answer the questions.

1. Which animals are mentioned? What can they do?
2. What is special about human communication? What can *we* do?
3. Which four forms of media are mentioned in the last paragraph?
4. What is good and bad about information technology today?

What do you think?

- What can animals do that people can't?
- How do *you* like to communicate?
- What is happening in information technology now?

PEOPLE
THE GREAT COMMUNICATORS

We can communicate with other people in many different ways. We can talk and write, and we can send messages with our hands and faces. There is also the telephone (including the cell phone!), the fax, and e-mail. Television, movies, painting, and photography can also communicate ideas.

Animals have ways of exchanging information, too. Bees dance and tell other bees where to find food. Elephants make sounds that humans can't hear. Whales sing songs. Monkeys use their faces to show anger and love. But this is nothing compared to what people can do. We have language—about 6,000 languages, in fact. We can write poetry, tell jokes, make promises, explain, persuade, tell the truth, or tell lies. And we have a sense of past and future, not just present.

Communication technologies were very important in the development of ancient societies:

- Around 2900 B.C., paper and hieroglyphics transformed Egyptian life.
- The ancient Greeks loved the spoken word. They were very good at public speaking, drama, and philosophy.
- The Romans developed a unique system of government that depended on the Roman alphabet.
- In the fifteenth century, the printing press helped develop new ways of thinking across Europe.

Radio, movies, and television have had a huge influence on society in the last hundred years. And now we have the Internet, which is infinite. But what is this doing to us? We can give and get a lot of information very quickly. But there is so much information that it is difficult to know what is important and what isn't. Modern media are changing our world every minute of every day.

LISTENING AND SPEAKING
Neighbors

1 What are your ideal neighbors like? Complete the questionnaire on the right, then discuss your answers with a partner.

2 "Good fences make good neighbors." What does this mean? Do you agree?

3 You will hear Mrs. Snell and her new neighbor, Steve, talking about each other.

Work in two groups.

T 1.4 **Group A** Listen to Mrs. Snell.

T 1.5 **Group B** Listen to Steve.

4 Answer the questions.

1. When did Steve move into his new apartment?
2. Is it a big apartment?
3. Who is staying with Steve at the moment?
4. Where does he work?
5. Does he work long hours?
6. What does he wear to work?
7. How many people came to the party?
8. What time did Steve's party end?
9. What is Steve doing tonight?

Compare your answers with a partner from the other group. What are the differences?

Role play

Work in groups of three.

Student A You are Steve.
Student B You are Mrs. Snell.
Student C You are another neighbor. You have invited Steve and Mrs. Snell to your apartment for coffee.

Make polite conversation. Talk about these things:

- Steve's job
- Steve's sister
- Steve's party

Neighbor	Do you two know each other?
Steve	Well, no. Not really.
Mrs. Snell	No.
Neighbor	Mrs. Snell, this is Steve James, our new neighbor. Steve, this is Mrs. Snell.
Steve	Nice to meet you, Mrs. Snell.
Mrs. Snell	Nice to meet you, Steve.
Neighbor	Steve works in advertising, you know ...

What do you think?

Write down three things that young people think about older people and three things that older people think about young people. In groups, compare ideas.

My ideal neighbors are people who ...

	Yes	No
... say hello when I see them.	☐	☐
... I never see.	☐	☐
... have parties and invite me.	☐	☐
... are very quiet.	☐	☐
... often come over for a cup of coffee.	☐	☐
... come over to borrow things.	☐	☐
... make themselves at home in my house.	☐	☐

EVERYDAY ENGLISH
Social expressions 1

1 We use certain expressions in different social situations.

> *I'm sorry I'm late!*

> *That's OK. Come in and sit down.*

Match the expressions and responses. When do we use these expressions?

1. How are you?	Sleep well!
2. Hello, Jane!	Yes. Can I help you?
3. See you tomorrow!	Good morning!
4. Good night!	Fine, thanks.
5. Good morning!	Nice to meet you, Elaine.
6. Hello, I'm Elaine Paul.	You're welcome.
7. Cheers!	Thanks.
8. Excuse me.	Same to you!
9. Make yourself at home.	Cheers!
10. Have a good weekend!	Bye! See you then.
11. Thank you very much.	Hi, Peter!
12. Bless you!	Thank you. That's very nice of you.

T 1.6 Listen and check. Practice saying the expressions.

2 Test a partner. Say an expression. Can your partner give the correct response?

3 With your partner, write two short conversations that include some of the social expressions. Read your conversations to the class.

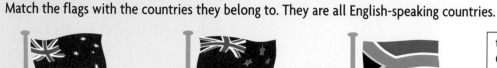

2 The way we live

Present tenses · *have* · **Collocation — daily life** · **Making conversation**

STARTER ▶ Match the flags with the countries they belong to. They are all English-speaking countries.

1. ___Australia___

3. _____

5. _____

| the United States |
| Canada |
| Australia |
| New Zealand |
| South Africa |
| the United Kingdom |

2. _____

4. _____

6. _____

PEOPLE AND PLACES
Present tenses

1 Complete each text with the words in the box. Then match a country from the Starter and a photograph to each text.

a ▢ | exports enjoy immigrants huge

This country has a fairly small population, just 16 million, but its area is **huge** . The people are mainly of European descent, but there are also aborigines and a lot of southeast Asian ____ . People live in towns on the coast, not so much inland, because it is so hot. They live a lot of their lives outdoors, and ____ sports, swimming, and having barbecues. This country ____ wine and wool—it has more than 60 million sheep!

b ▢ | popular variety has only

This is the second biggest country in the world, but it has a population of ____ 30 million. It is so big that there is a ____ of climates. Most people live in the south because the north is too cold. It is famous for its beautiful mountains and lakes—it ____ more lakes than any other country. Two of the most ____ sports are ice hockey and baseball.

c ▢ | elephants grows black climate

This country has a population of about 45 million. Of these, 76 percent are ____ and 12 percent white. It has a warm ____ . Either it never rains, or it rains a lot! It is the world's biggest producer of gold, and it exports diamonds, too. It ____ a lot of fruit, including oranges, pears, and grapes, and it makes wine. In the game reserves you can see a lot of wildlife, including lions, ____ , zebras, and giraffes.

2 **T 2.1** Listen to three people describing the other countries. Match a country and photograph with each description.

 d [ ]   e [ ]   f [ ]

3 Close your books. Can you remember three facts about each country? Tell a partner.

4 Give some similar facts about your country.

PRACTICE

Talking about you

1 Practice the forms of the Present Simple in the question, short answer, and negative.

   1. have a computer/a car

> *Do you have a computer?*

> *Yes, I do.*

> *Do you have a car?*

> *No, I don't. I just have a bicycle.*

   2. your father work in an office?

> *Does your father work in an office?*

> *No, he doesn't. He works in a school. He's a teacher ...*

T 2.2 Listen and repeat.

2 Ask and answer questions about these things with a partner.

- have a cell phone/a credit card/a pet?
- sometimes wear jeans/sneakers/a hat?
- drink tea/coffee/wine?
- your family live in an apartment?
- your grandmother live near you?
- your sister/brother have a boyfriend/girlfriend?

Tell the class some things about your partner.

> *Roberto has a cell phone, but he doesn't have a computer. He ...*

3 Practice the Present Continuous. What are you doing now? What is your teacher doing?

Are you ...	Is she/he ...		
... sitting down?	... standing up?	... talking?	... writing?
... smiling?	... laughing?	... working hard?	

Talk to your partner.

> *I'm sitting down and I'm working very hard. My teacher's laughing!*

4 Write questions to find the information about the people on the right.

City/country	• Where does he ... from?
Family	• ... she married?
	• ... they have any ... ?
	• How many brothers and sisters ... she ... ?
Occupation	• What ... he do?
Free time/vacation	• What ... she ... in her free time?
	• Where ... they go on vacation?
Current activity	• What ... she doing right now?

T 2.3 Listen and check.

Getting information

5 Work with a partner.

   Student A Go to page 115.
   Student B Go to page 117.

6 Think of questions to ask about free time and vacation activities.

- What do you do in your free time?
- What do ... on weekends?
- ... any sports?
- Do you ... any hobbies?
- Do you like ... ?
- Where ... vacation?

Stand up! Ask three students your questions. Use short answers when necessary. Find out who has the most hobbies and best vacations.

 *Do you like skiing?*   *No, I don't.*

Check it

7 Put a check (✓) next to the correct sentence.

1. ☐ Where you go on vacation?
   ☐ Where do you go on vacation?
2. ☐ I'm Yaling. I'm coming from Taiwan.
   ☐ I'm Yaling. I come from Taiwan.
3. ☐ This is a great party! Everyone is dancing.
   ☐ This is a great party! Everyone dances.
4. ☐ I don't have a cell phone.
   ☐ I no have a cell phone.
5. ☐ Jack's a police officer, but he doesn't wear a uniform.
   ☐ Jack's a police officer, but he no wear a uniform.
6. ☐ "Where is Pete?" "He's sitting by the window."
   ☐ "Where is Pete?" "He sits by the window."
7. ☐ I'm liking black coffee.
   ☐ I like black coffee.

VOCABULARY
Daily life

1 Match the verbs and nouns.

have	a movie on TV
wash	to my friends
watch	my hair
talk	breakfast

make	to music
listen	my homework
relax	some coffee
do	on the sofa

take	posters on the wall
clean up	the mess
do	a shower
have/put	the dishes

cook	magazines
go	a meal
put on	makeup
read	to the bathroom

T 2.4 Listen and check.

2 Match the activities from Exercise 1 with the correct room.

Kitchen
_____
_____
_____
_____

Bathroom
_____
_____
_____

Living room
_____
_____

Bedroom
_____
_____

3 Do you like where you live? Choose your favorite room. What do you do in that room?

I like my bedroom a lot because I have lots of posters on the walls. I listen to music and do my homework ...

I like my living room. The walls are white, and I love the big, comfortable sofa ...

4 Describe your favorite room to a partner. Don't say which room it is. Can your partner guess?

READING AND SPEAKING
Living in the USA

1 Close your eyes and think of the United States. Write down the first five things you think of.

The Empire State Building
Cheeseburgers and fries

Compare your list with other students.

2 Read the introduction to the magazine article. Then work in three groups.

Group A Read about Roberto.
Group B Read about Endre.
Group C Read about Yuet.

3 Answer the questions.

1. Why and when did he/she come to the United States?
2. What does he/she do?
3. What does he/she like about living in the United States?
4. What was difficult at the beginning?

4 Find a partner from each of the other two groups. Compare the three people.

5 Answer the questions with your group.

1. What do the people have in common?
2. Are they all happy living in the United States?
3. Who has other members of their family living in the United States?
4. Do they all have children?
5. Who married someone from their own country?
6. What do Roberto and Endre like about the United States?
7. What do they say about their own country?
8. Do they like the people in the United States?
9. What do they say about Americans and their cars?

What do you think?

- What do you like best about living in your country? What would you miss if you lived abroad?

- Do you know any foreigners living in your country? What do they like about it? What do they say is different?

LIVING IN

Every year, tens of thousands of people from around the world travel to the United States to study or visit. But what is it like to live there? How do people like the US when they first arrive? What do they think of the people and the way of life?

Jeff Peterson spoke to three people.

THE USA

Roberto Solano
from Mexico

Endre Boros
from Hungary

Yuet Tung
from Hong Kong

Roberto came from Mexico to New York ten years ago. At first he missed everything—the sunshine, the food, his girlfriend. But now he has a successful business with his three brothers and his sister. They run a soccer store in a small town near New York City. Roberto's girlfriend is now his wife, and they have two children.

When asked why he came to the United States, Roberto says without hesitation, "Because I want to work hard and have my own business." He certainly works hard. He's at the store all day, then works as a driver in the evening. "That's why I like America," he says. "You can be whatever you want."

"When I first came here, I only spoke Spanish. Then I went to high school and learned English. The people were friendly, but I missed my family. Now nearly all my family are here. We meet about once a month and have a huge Mexican meal that takes about five hours! We're all happy here."

Endre is a professor at Rutgers University in New Jersey. He came from Budapest 13 years ago. "I had an opportunity to come here for two years." After a year, his wife came to join him, and since then they've had a daughter, so they decided to stay.

"At first it was very strange. Everything is so big here," he says. "I started to feel happy when I bought a car. Now I go everywhere by car. In Hungary, we only use the car on weekends, but here your car is part of your life. Nobody walks anywhere."

What does he think of the people? "Very friendly. The first question everybody asks you is 'Where are you from?' People talk to you here, they start conversations."

What about the way of life? "The thing I like best is the independence. Nobody tells me what to do. Here you can do what you want, so you learn to make decisions for yourself. I feel in control."

Yuet is her Chinese name, but in English she's known as Clara. She came to the United States eight years ago and studied fine art. Now she works on Madison Avenue for a publishing company. She married a Vietnamese American three years ago, and they live in a suburb of New York. They don't have any children yet.

How does she like working in New York? "It's very similar to Hong Kong. It's a busy city, very exciting, and people walk very fast! I like the stores here. They're huge, and it's cheaper than Hong Kong. In Hong Kong everyone uses public transportation because it's good and it's cheap. But you need a car here. At first I hated driving, but it's OK now."

What does she like best? "The space. Here I live in a house with a yard. In Hong Kong it is so crowded. And the people here are friendly. When I go jogging, everyone says 'Hi!' And the food is from every country in the world."

LISTENING AND SPEAKING
You drive me crazy (but I love you)!

1 Complete these sentences about the people in your life. Tell a partner.

- My mother/father drives me crazy when she/he ...
- I hate it when my boyfriend/girlfriend ...
- I don't like friends who ...
- It really annoys me when people ...

Dave and Alison

2 Choose one person in your life. What annoying habits does he/she have?

Does he/she ... ?
- always arrive late
- talk too loudly
- leave things on the floor

Is he/she ... ?
- messy
- always on the phone
- never on time

Mike and Carol

What annoying habits do *you* have? Discuss with your partner.

3 You are going to listen to a radio program called *Home Truths*. Two couples, Carol and Mike, and Dave and Alison, talk about their partner's annoying habits. Look at the pictures below. What are their annoying habits?

T 2.5 Listen and write the correct name under each picture below.

1 Alison
3
5
7

2
4
6
8

4 Are these sentences true (✓) or false (✗)? Correct the false sentences.

1. Carol and Mike never watch television.
2. Mike doesn't listen when his wife speaks to him.
3. Carol makes the decisions in their house.
4. Mike asks his wife for directions whenever he's driving.
5. Dave never does any jobs at home.
6. Dave is bad at his job.
7. Dave is very messy.
8. Alison is usually on time.

What do you think?

1 Do men or women typically complain about their partners doing these things?

- watching sports on TV
- telling the other how to drive
- taking a long time to get ready
- being messy

2 What do you think men are generally better at? What are women better at?

EVERYDAY ENGLISH
Making conversation

1 **T 2.6** Listen to two conversations. Maria and Sergio are foreign students in the United States. Their teachers are trying to be friendly. Which conversation is more successful? Why?

2 Obviously, it is impossible to tell someone how to have a conversation, but here are some things that help.

- Ask questions.
- Show that you're interested.
- Don't just answer *yes* or *no*.
- Try to add a comment of your own.
- Don't let the conversation stop.

Find examples of these points in the tapescript on page 129.

3 Match a line in **A** with a reply in **B** and a further comment in **C**.

A	B	C
1. What a nice day it is today!	I'm enjoying it.	What was the score?
2. How are you today?	Yes, no problems.	We went to the beach and did some shopping.
3. Did you have a nice weekend?	Fine, thanks.	The plane was a little late, but it didn't matter.
4. How do you like living in Texas?	No, I missed it.	I got it in San Francisco last year.
5. Did you have a good flight?	Thank you.	How about you?
6. Did you watch the soccer game yesterday?	Yes.	It was kind of strange at first, but I'm getting used to it.
7. What a beautiful coat you're wearing!	Yes, we had a great time.	It's beautiful, isn't it?

T 2.7 Listen and check. Practice the conversations with a partner.

4 Think of three questions to ask someone about each of these subjects.

- job • home • free time • last vacation

5 Invent a new name and background for yourself.

> *My name's James Bond. I'm a spy. I have homes in London, Moscow, and Beijing …*

Stand up! You're all at a party. Try to make some friends.

3 It all went wrong

Past tenses · Word formation · Time expressions

STARTER Here are the past tense forms of some irregular verbs. Write the present tenses.

1. <u>are</u> were
2. _____ saw
3. _____ went
4. _____ told
5. _____ said
6. _____ had
7. _____ took
8. _____ gave
9. _____ got
10. _____ could
11. _____ made
12. _____ did

THE BURGLARS' FRIEND
Past Simple

1 **T 3.1** Read and listen to the newspaper article. Why was Russell the burglars' friend?

The Burglars' Friend

His parents were fast asleep in bed

IT WAS 3 O'CLOCK IN THE morning when four-year-old Russell Brown woke up to go to the bathroom.

His parents were fast asleep in bed. But when he heard a noise in the living room and saw a light was on, he went downstairs.

There he found two men. They asked him his name and told him they were friends of the family.

Unfortunately, Russell believed them. They asked him where the VCR and TV were. Russell showed them and said they had a stereo and CD player, too.

The two men carried these to the kitchen. Russell also told them that his mother kept her wallet in a drawer in the kitchen, so they took that. Russell even gave them his pocket money—50 cents.

They finally left at 4 A.M. They said, "Will you open the back door while we take these things to the car, because we don't want to wake Mommy and Daddy, OK?" So Russell held the door open for them. He then went back to bed.

His parents didn't know about the burglary until they got up the next day. His father said, "I couldn't be angry with Russell because he thought he was doing the right thing."

Fortunately, the police caught the two burglars last week.

2 Write the past forms of these irregular verbs from the article.

wake <u>woke</u>   leave _____

hear _____   hold _____

find _____   think _____

keep _____   catch _____

3 `T 3.2` You will hear some sentences about the story. Correct the mistakes.

Russell woke up at 2 o'clock.

> *He didn't wake up at 2:00! He woke up at 3:00.*

4 Write the questions to these answers.

1. Because he wanted to go to the bathroom.
   Why did he wake up?
2. They were in bed.
3. Because he heard a noise and saw a light on.
4. Two.
5. They told him they were friends of the family.
6. In a drawer in the kitchen.
7. Fifty cents.
8. At 4 A.M.
9. The next day. *(When ... find out about ... ?)*
10. Last week.

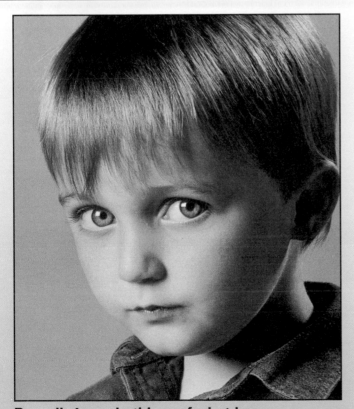

Russell, 4, made thieves feel at home

GRAMMAR SPOT

1 What tense are nearly all the verbs in the article? Why? How do we form the question and negative?

2 Write the Past Simple of these verbs.

   a. ask   <u>asked</u>   c. like   _____
   show _____   believe _____
   want _____   use _____
   walk _____
   start _____

   b. try _____   d. stop _____
   carry _____   plan _____

`T 3.3` Listen and repeat.

3 How is the regular past tense formed?
How is the past tense formed when the verb ends in a consonant + *y*?
When do we double the final consonant?
There is a list of irregular verbs on page 153.

▶▶ **Grammar Reference 3.1 p. 141**

PRACTICE

Making connections

1 Match the verb phrases. Then make sentences using both verbs in the past. Join the sentences with *so*, *because*, *and*, or *but*.

I broke a cup, but I fixed it with glue.

1. break a cup	answer it
2. feel sick	fix it
3. make a sandwich	wash my hair
4. take a shower	laugh
5. lose my passport	be hungry
6. call the police	go to bed
7. run out of coffee	buy some more
8. forget her birthday	find it
9. phone ring	say I was sorry
10. tell a joke	hear a strange noise

`T 3.4` Listen and compare your answers.

Talking about you

2 Ask and answer these questions with a partner. Make more questions using the Past Simple.

What did you do ... ?
- last night
- last weekend
- on your last birthday
- on your last vacation

> *I watched TV.*

> *I went swimming.*

NEWSPAPER STORIES

Past Continuous

1 Read each text and <u>underline</u> the Past Simple of the verbs in the boxes.

| have | can | steal | give | say |

| break | hear | come | leave | go |

a

Hands up, I've got a burger!

Last Tuesday a man armed with just a hot hamburger in a bag <u>stole</u> $1,000 from a bank in Danville, California. Police Detective Bill McGinnis said that the robber (1) _____ , entered the Mount Diablo National Bank at about 1:30 P.M. and gave the teller a note demanding $1,000. He claimed that he had a bomb in the bag. The teller said she could smell a distinct odor of hamburger coming from the bag. Even so, she handed the money to the man. (2) _____ , he dropped the bag with the hamburger. He escaped in a car (3) _____ .

Police Detective Bill McGinnis

b

Teenage party ends in tears

When Jack and Kelly Harman went away on vacation, they left their teenage daughter alone in the house. Sue, aged 16, wanted to stay at home (4) _____ . Her parents said she could have some friends stay over. However, Sue decided to have a party. (5) _____ things started to go wrong. Forty uninvited guests arrived (6) _____ . They broke furniture, smashed windows, and stole jewelry. When Mr. and Mrs. Harman heard the news, they came home immediately.

Sue Harman, 16, home alone

2 Match each phrase to an article. Where exactly does each phrase go?

because she was studying for a test

as he was running out of the bank

everyone was having a good time when suddenly

that was waiting for him outside

and some of them were carrying knives

who was wearing a mask

T 3.5 Listen and check. Practice the sentences.

GRAMMAR SPOT

1 The verb forms in Exercise 2 are in the Past Continuous. Complete the forms of the Past Continuous.

I **was studying** .   We _____ waiting.
You _____ studying.   They _____ waiting.
She _____ studying.

2 Look at these sentences. What's the difference between them?

| When we arrived, | she made
she was making | some coffee. |

▶▶ **Grammar Reference 3.2 and 3.3 p. 142**

PRACTICE

Discussing grammar

1 Choose the correct verb form.

1. I (*saw*)/ *was seeing* a very good program on TV last night.
2. While I *shopped / was shopping* this morning, I *lost / was losing* my wallet. I don't know how.
3. Last week the police *stopped / were stopping* Alan in his car because he *drove / was driving* at over 120 kilometers an hour.
4. How *did you cut / were you cutting* your finger?
5. I *cooked / was cooking* and I *dropped / was dropping* the knife.
6. When I *arrived / was arriving* at the party, everyone *had / was having* a good time.
7. *Did you have / Were you having* a good time on your vacation last month?

2 Complete the sentences with the verbs in the Past Simple or Past Continuous.

1. While I **was going** (go) to work this morning, I _____ (meet) an old friend.
2. I _____ (not want) to get up this morning. It _____ (rain) and it was cold, and my bed was so warm.
3. I _____ (listen) to the news on the radio when the phone _____ (ring).
4. But when I _____ (pick) up the phone, there was no one there.
5. I _____ (say) "Hello" to the children, but they didn't say anything because they _____ (watch) television.

Getting information

3 Work with a partner. You will each have information about the teenage party, but you don't have all the information. Ask and answer questions.

Student A Go to page 118.
Student B Go to page 120.

fortunately/unfortunately

4 Continue this story around the class.

I went out for a walk.
Unfortunately, it began to rain.
Fortunately, I had an umbrella.
Unfortunately, it was broken.
Fortunately, I met a friend in his car.
Unfortunately, his car ran out of gas.
Fortunately, ...

5 Tell similar stories around the class. Begin with these sentences.

- I lost my wallet yesterday.
- It was my birthday last week.
- We went out for dinner last night.
- I went on vacation to ... last year.

LISTENING AND READING
A spy story

1 Who is James Bond? Write down anything you know about him and share ideas with the class.

2 The following are titles of James Bond movies. Have you seen any of these movies?

Goldfinger
From Russia with Love
The Man with the Golden Gun
The Spy Who Loved Me
GoldenEye
Tomorrow Never Dies

Do you know any more James Bond movies?

Do you know the translation of any of the titles in your language?

3 **T 3.6** You are going to listen to an extract from *The Man with the Golden Gun*. Cover the story on page 23 and look at the pictures. What can you guess about the story? Then listen and answer the questions below.

1. Who are the people in the pictures? Where are they?
2. How did Mary get into the room?
3. Why did she come to find James Bond?
4. Where did they go to talk?
5. What did Scaramanga say? What did he do?
6. Who has the golden gun?

4 Read the story. Find the lines in the text that go with each picture.

The Man with the Golden Gun

James Bond got back to his hotel room at midnight. The windows were closed and the air conditioner was on. Bond switched it off and opened the windows. His heart was still thumping in his chest. He breathed in the air with relief, then he took a shower and went to bed.

At 3:30 he was dreaming, not very peacefully, about three black-coated men with red eyes and angry white teeth. Suddenly he woke up. He listened. There was a noise. It was coming from the window. Someone was moving behind the curtain. James Bond took his gun from under his pillow, got quietly out of bed, and crept slowly along the wall toward the window. Someone was breathing behind the curtain. Bond pulled it back with one quick movement. Golden hair shone in the moonlight.

"Mary Goodnight!" Bond exclaimed. "What are *you* doing here?"

"Quick, James! Help me in!" Mary whispered urgently. Bond put down his gun and tried to pull her through the open window. At the last moment the window banged shut with a noise like a gunshot.

"I'm really sorry, James!" Mary Goodnight whispered.

"Shh! Shh!" said Bond. He quickly led her across the room to the bathroom. First he turned on the light, then the shower. They sat down on the side of the bathtub.

"Mary," Bond asked again. "What on earth are you doing here? What's the matter?"

"James, I was so worried. An urgent message came from HQ this evening. A top KGB man, using the name Hendriks, is staying in this hotel. He knows you're here. He's looking for you!"

"I know," said Bond. "Hendriks is here all right. So is a gunman named Scaramanga. Mary, did HQ say if they have a description of me?"

"No, they don't. They just have your name, Secret Agent James Bond."

"Thanks, Mary. Now, I have to get you out of here. Don't worry about me. Just tell HQ that you gave me the message, OK?"

"OK, James." Mary Goodnight stood up and looked into his eyes. "Please be careful, James."

"Sure, sure." Bond turned off the shower and opened the bathroom door. "Now, come on!"

Suddenly a voice came from the darkness of the bedroom. "This is not your lucky day, Mr. Bond. Come here, both of you, and put your hands up!"

Scaramanga walked to the door and turned on the lights. His golden gun was pointing directly at James Bond.

5 Are these sentences true (✓) or false (✗)? Correct the false sentences.

1. James Bond felt happy to be back in his hotel room.
2. Bond was dreaming about Mary Goodnight.
3. A man with a gun woke Bond at 3:30 A.M.
4. He was very pleased to see Mary Goodnight.
5. Bond fired his gun while he was pulling Mary through the window.
6. They talked while the shower was running.
7. Bond knew that Hendriks was looking for him.
8. James helped Mary get out of the hotel.

What do you think?

- What was James Bond doing before he got back to his hotel room?
- Why did James and Mary talk in the bathroom?
- Does Mary Goodnight like James a lot?
- Does Scaramanga kill James Bond and Mary? What do you think happens next?

Language work

6 Write the past form of these verbs from the story. Which are irregular?

1. get _____got_____
2. breathe _____
3. wake up _____
4. take _____
5. creep _____
6. shine _____
7. whisper _____
8. put _____
9. try _____
10. lead _____
11. give _____
12. stand up _____

7 What do these colors refer to in the story?

| black white red golden |

Telling the story

8 Use the pictures to tell the story to a partner in your own words.

VOCABULARY

Nouns, verbs, and adjectives

1 Look at these common noun and adjective suffixes. These suffixes can be used to form different parts of speech.

Nouns	-ation -ion -ness -ity -ence -sion -ment
Adjectives	-ous -y -tific -ly -ful -less -ial

Complete the charts below and mark the stress. There are some spelling changes.

Noun	Verb
communi'cation	co'mmunicate
_____	dis'cuss
_____	'govern
invi'tation	_____
_____	de'velop
_____	ex'plain
edu'cation	_____
_____	de'cide
_____	en'joy
_____	'organize
im'provement	_____
_____	em'ploy

Noun	Adjective
'science	scien'tific
friend	_____
_____	'happy
_____	'different
'danger	_____
use	_____
help	_____
_____	'special
care	_____
noise	_____
'industry	_____
am'bition	_____

2 Complete each sentence with a word from Exercise 1.

1. My English **improved** a lot after I lived in Toronto for a month.
2. I have two _____ in life. I want to be rich, and I want to be famous.
3. "I'm going to work hard from now on." "That's a very good _____ ."
4. There are many _____ between my two children. They aren't similar at all.
5. Thank you for your advice. It was very _____ .
6. I like Italian people. They're very nice and _____ .
7. The United Nations is an international _____ .
8. I asked the teacher for help, but unfortunately I didn't understand his _____ .
9. Auto racing is a very _____ sport.
10. Fish soup is a _____ of this area. You must try it.
11. I'm having a party on Saturday, and I'd like to _____ you.
12. This is the _____ part of my town. There are lots of factories and businesses here.

Making negatives

3 We can make adjectives and verbs negative by using these prefixes.

Adjectives	un- im- in- il-
Verbs	un- dis-

Complete the sentences, using a word from the box and a prefix.

pack possible agree lock fair like
appear employed legal polite

1. This key doesn't work! I can't **unlock** the door.
2. I can't do math. For me, it's an _____ subject.
3. I don't _____ fish. I just prefer meat.
4. It's very _____ to ask someone how much they make.
5. When we arrived at the hotel, we _____ our suitcases.
6. I was _____ for two years. Finally, I got a job.
7. "I think learning languages is stupid." "I _____ . I think it's a good idea."
8. The thief stole my bag, ran into the crowd, and _____ . I never saw him again.
9. It's _____ to drive a car without a driver's license.
10. You gave her more money than me! That's _____ !

EVERYDAY ENGLISH
Time expressions

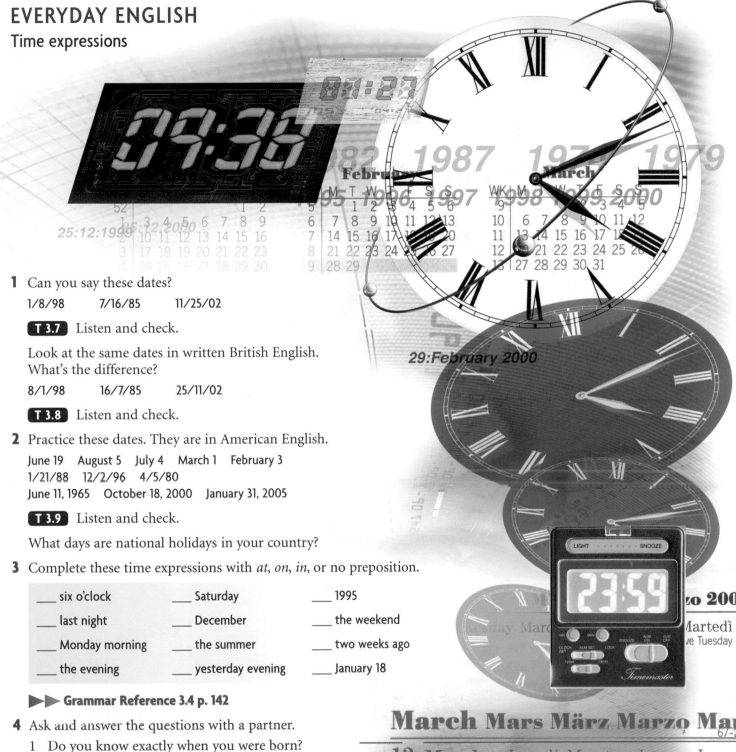

1 Can you say these dates?

1/8/98   7/16/85   11/25/02

T 3.7 Listen and check.

Look at the same dates in written British English. What's the difference?

8/1/98   16/7/85   25/11/02

T 3.8 Listen and check.

2 Practice these dates. They are in American English.

June 19   August 5   July 4   March 1   February 3
1/21/88   12/2/96   4/5/80
June 11, 1965   October 18, 2000   January 31, 2005

T 3.9 Listen and check.

What days are national holidays in your country?

3 Complete these time expressions with *at*, *on*, *in*, or no preposition.

___ six o'clock	___ Saturday	___ 1995
___ last night	___ December	___ the weekend
___ Monday morning	___ the summer	___ two weeks ago
___ the evening	___ yesterday evening	___ January 18

▶▶ **Grammar Reference 3.4 p. 142**

4 Ask and answer the questions with a partner.

1   Do you know exactly when you were born?

> *I was born at two o'clock in the morning on Monday, June twenty-fifth, 1979.*

2   When did you last … ?
- go to the movies
- play a sport
- give someone a present
- take a vacation
- watch TV
- go to a party
- take a test
- see a lot of snow
- brush your teeth
- take a plane trip

4 Let's go shopping!

much/many · some/any · a few, a little, a lot of · Articles · Shopping · Prices

STARTER

Play the alphabet game with things you can buy. Continue around the class.

A Yesterday I went shopping, and I bought an **a**pple.
B Yesterday I went shopping ,and I bought an **a**pple and some **b**read.
C Yesterday I went shopping, and I bought an **a**pple, some **b**read, and ...

THE WEEKEND SHOPPING TRIP
Quantity

1 Sarah and Vicky are two students who share an apartment. It is Saturday morning, and Sarah has a shopping list.

T 4.1 Read and listen to the first part of their conversation.

V It says here *milk*. How much milk do we need?
S Two liters.
V And eggs? How many eggs?
S A dozen.
V And what about potatoes? How many potatoes?
S A kilo's enough.
V And butter? How much?
S Just one package.

milk — cheese
eggs — soda
potatoes — frozen pizzas
butter — jam
bread — potato chips
tomatoes

GRAMMAR SPOT

Can we count butter?
Can we count eggs? (one egg, two eggs)
When do we say *How much ... ?*
When do we say *How many ... ?*

▶▶ **Grammar Reference 4.1 p. 143**

---

2 Match these quantifiers with the items from the shopping list.

bread	200g of cheddar
tomatoes	a jar
cheese	just one loaf
soda	a bag
frozen pizzas	four or five big ones
jam	three bottles
potato chips	one pepperoni, one plain

Continue the conversation with a partner.

3 **T 4.2** Read and listen to the rest of Sarah and Vicky's conversation.

V Do we need anything else?

S Let's see. We have some apples, but there aren't any grapes. And there isn't any coffee, but we have some tea.

V Is there any orange juice left, or did somebody finish it?

S There's a little, but there isn't much, so we need some more.

V And vegetables? Do we have many vegetables?

S Well, I see a lot of carrots, but there aren't many onions.

V Don't forget we need a lot of potato chips and soda. My nephews are coming tomorrow!

S OK. I think that's everything. Let's go! By the way, how much money do you have? Can I borrow some?

GRAMMAR SPOT

1 Find seven count nouns (CNs) and five noncount nouns (NCs) in Exercise 3.

2 Put a check (✓) in the correct columns.

We use . . .	with CNs	with NCs	in affirmative sentences	in questions	in negative sentences
some any much many	✓	✓	✓	✓ (sometimes)	✗
lots/a lot of a few a little	✓	✓	✓	✓	✓

3 Look at the forms of *something/someone,* etc. The rules are the same as for *some* and *any* above. Find three examples in Exercise 3.

some any	+	thing one/body where

▶▶ **Grammar Reference 4.1 on p. 143**

PRACTICE

Discussing grammar

1 Complete the sentences with *some* or *any*.

1. Do you have __any__ brothers or sisters?
2. We don't need _____ olive oil.
3. Here are _____ letters for you.
4. I need _____ money.
5. There aren't _____ tomatoes left.

2 Complete the sentences with *much* or *many*.

1. Do you have _____ homework?
2. We don't need _____ eggs. Just half a dozen.
3. Is there _____ traffic in your town?
4. I don't know _____ students in this class.
5. How _____ people live in your house?

3 Complete the sentences with *a little*, *a few*, or *a lot of*.

1. I have _____ close friends. Two or three.
2. He has _____ money. He's a millionaire.
3. "Do you take sugar in your coffee?" "Just _____ . Half a spoonful."
4. "Do you have _____ CDs?" "Yes, hundreds."
5. I'll be ready in _____ minutes.
6. She speaks good Spanish, but only _____ Portuguese.

Questions and answers

4 Look at Sarah and Vicky's bathroom. Ask and answer questions with a partner about these things:

- makeup
- shampoo
- towels
- toothbrushes
- toothpaste
- toilet paper
- hairbrushes
- soap
- bottles of perfume

> *Do they have much makeup?*
>
> *Lots.*
>
> *Is there any soap?*
>
> *I can't see any.*

28 Unit 4 · Let's go shopping!

something/someone/somewhere

5 Complete the sentences with the correct word.

some any every no	+	thing one/body where

1. "Did you meet __anyone__ nice at the party?"
   "Yes. I met _____ who knows you!"
2. "Ouch! There's _____ in my eye!"
   "Let me look. No, I can't see _____ ."
3. "Let's go _____ nice for our vacation."
   "But we can't go _____ that's too expensive."
4. "I'm so unhappy. _____ loves me."
   "I know _____ who loves you. Me."
5. I lost my glasses. I looked _____ , but I couldn't find them.
6. "Did you buy _____ when you were shopping?"
   "No, _____ . I didn't have any money."
7. I'm bored. I want _____ interesting to read, or _____ interesting to talk to, or _____ interesting to go.
8. It was a great party. _____ loved it.

T 4.3 Listen and check.

Town survey

6 Work in groups. Talk about the good things and bad things about living in your city or town. Make a list. Compare your list with the class.

> Good things
>
> There are a lot of cafes and restaurants.
>
> There are some good stores.
>
> We can go on lots of walks.
>
> Bad things
>
> But we don't have any good clubs.
>
> There aren't many ...
>
> There's only one ...
>
> There isn't anywhere that we can ...

THE HAPPIEST MAN I KNOW

My uncle owns a general store in a small town north of Boston. The store sells a lot of things—bread, milk, fruit, vegetables, newspapers, tools, videotapes—almost everything! It is also the town post office. The children in the town always stop to buy candy or ice cream on their way home from school.

My uncle doesn't go out of town very often. He doesn't like to drive, so once a month he goes by bus to the next town and has lunch at a nice restaurant with some friends. He is one of the happiest men I know.

Articles

T 4.4 Read and listen to the text.

> ### GRAMMAR SPOT
>
> 1 Find examples of the definite article (*the*) + noun and the indefinite article (*a/an*) + noun.
> 2 Find examples of nouns without an article. (*bread, candy*)
>
> ▶▶ **Grammar Reference 4.2 p. 143**

PRACTICE

Discussing grammar

1 In pairs, find one mistake in each sentence.
1. He's mail carrier, so he has breakfast at 4 A.M.
   He's a mail carrier, so he has breakfast at 4 a.m.
2. The love is more important than money.
3. I come to school by the bus.
4. I live in one old house in the country.
5. "Where's Jack?" "In a kitchen."
6. I live in center of town, near the hospital.
7. My parents moved to a new apartment in country.
8. I don't eat the bread because I don't like it.

2 Complete the sentences with *a/an*, *the*, or nothing.
1. I have two children, __*a*__ boy and _____ girl. _____ boy is 22 and _____ girl is 19.
2. Mike is _____ soldier in _____ army, and Linda is in _____ college.
3. My wife goes to _____ work by _____ train. She's _____ accountant. I don't have _____ job. I stay _____ home and take care of _____ children.
4. What _____ beautiful day! Why don't we go for _____ picnic in _____ park?
5. "What did you have for _____ lunch?" "Just _____ sandwich."

READING

The best shopping street in the world

1 Match a famous shopping street with a city, a store, and a product.

Street	City	Store	Product
Fifth Avenue	Hong Kong	Guerlain	sweaters
Champs-Elysées	London	Tiffany's	silk
Oxford Street	New York	Shanghai Tang	jewelry
Pedder Street	Paris	Marks and Spencer	perfume

2 Read the headline and the first paragraph of the newspaper article on page 31. Does anything surprise you? What do you want to find out when you read the article? Write some questions.

3 Read the article quickly and answer the questions you wrote in Exercise 2 above.

What is the best summary of the article?

Nowy Swiat is the best shopping street in the world because …
☐ … so many Polish people go walking there.
☐ … it is a pleasant place to go shopping, and the stores are small.
☐ … everything is very expensive and very exclusive.
☐ … the stores sell quality goods that you can't buy anywhere else.

4 Read the article again and answer the questions.

1. How do we know that Nowy Swiat is the most popular shopping street?
2. Why is it such a nice place to go shopping?
3. What can you see in the photos that is described in the article?
4. Why don't a lot of foreign people go to Nowy Swiat?
5. Why are the things produced by Polish manufacturers so good?
6. What can you buy here? What can't you buy?
7. What is expensive? What isn't expensive?
8. What's good about *Cafe Blikle*?
9. What is special about the stores on Nowy Swiat?

Language work

Complete the sentences with two different ideas from the article.

On Nowy Swiat, there are a lot of …   *There isn't any …*
There aren't any/many …   *There are some …*

What do you think?

- What are some of the famous brands and products that you can buy in many countries of the world? Think of clothes, food, cars, etc. Make a list. Work in groups and choose the most famous three. Compare your list with the class.

- What is the main shopping street in your city or town? What can you buy there that's special?

- Do you enjoy shopping? What do you like shopping for? What *don't* you like shopping for?

The best shopping street in the world

No, it isn't Oxford Street, the Champs-Elysées, or even Fifth Avenue. A new survey shows that the most popular shopping street in the world is … Nowy Swiat. Where's that? In Warsaw, Poland, of course.

by ANNE APPLEBAUM

"If you're tired, stop at Cafe Blikle."

"There are a lot of small, chic shops."

A recent survey has shown that the busiest shopping street in the world is not in London, New York, or Paris, but in Warsaw. It's called Nowy Swiat (pronounced /ˈnɑvi ʃviət/) which means *New World*. An incredible 14,000 Poles walk down this main street every hour.

It is a wonderful place to shop. The sidewalks are very wide. There are statues, palaces, attractive townhouses, exclusive cafes, and stylish restaurants. The buildings aren't too tall. They look old, but in fact the whole city was rebuilt after World War II.

There aren't any billboards or neon lights. There isn't any loud music, and there aren't many tourists. People think that Polish stores have nothing to sell, so nobody goes shopping here. The world doesn't know about this paradise for shoppers—yet.

It is now possible to buy almost everything in Warsaw. There are a lot of stores from the West, but the interesting thing is that Polish manufacturers are now producing high quality goods. They are good because they are not mass produced for world consumption.

Nowy Swiat has a lot of small stores, specialty stores, chic stores. It doesn't have the huge department stores that sell the same things everywhere.

If you want an exquisite handmade suit, Nowy Swiat is the place to go. It isn't cheap. You will pay up to $2,000. For beautiful French baby clothes, go to *Petit Bateau*. You will pay $75 for a pair of baby blue jeans. A dress for a baby girl is about $150. At *Désa*, a famous antique store, a desk costs $8,000, and a nineteenth century Russian icon is $300.

Not everything is expensive. At a store called *Pantera* you can buy leather goods—handbags, purses, coats, and belts. *Cepelia* specializes in folk art. There are also bookstores and record stores. And there are a lot of small boutiques that sell men's and women's clothes that aren't too expensive.

If you're tired, stop at *Cafe Blikle*. This is a fashionable place to meet. You'll find a lively atmosphere and a lot of well-known Poles. The frozen yogurt and ice cream are both excellent, and its famous doughnuts are delicious.

It is possible to travel the world and find the same things for sale in every country. But Warsaw is different because its stores are unique—and they're on Nowy Swiat.

VOCABULARY AND LISTENING
Buying things

1 What can you buy or do in these places? Write two more things for each place.
Compare your ideas with the class.

a cafe	a clothing store	a bank	a newsstand	a drugstore
drink coffee	buy jeans	exchange money	buy a magazine	buy makeup

2 **T 4.5** You will hear four conversations. Listen to each conversation and answer the questions.
1. Where is the conversation taking place? Choose from one of the places in Exercise 1.
2. What does the customer want?
3. Can the sales clerk/cashier help?
4. How much does the customer pay?

3 Complete these lines from the conversations. Look at the tapescript on page 130 and check your answers.

1. **A** Hello. Can I help you?
   B I _____ , thanks.
   …
   B I'm looking for a sweater _____ . Do you have _____ ?
   A I'll take a look. _____ are you?
   B Medium.

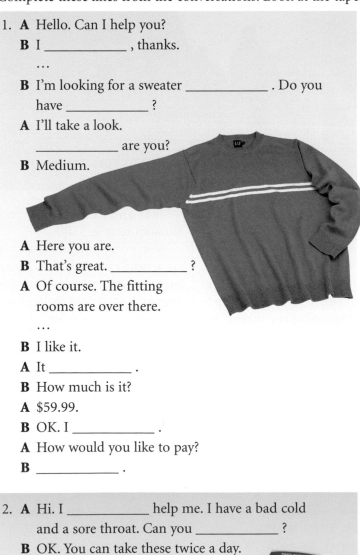

   A Here you are.
   B That's great. _____ ?
   A Of course. The fitting rooms are over there.
   …
   B I like it.
   A It _____ .
   B How much is it?
   A $59.99.
   B OK. I _____ .
   A How would you like to pay?
   B _____ .

2. **A** Hi. I _____ help me. I have a bad cold and a sore throat. Can you _____ ?
   B OK. You can take these twice a day.
   A Thank you. _____ some tissues _____ ?
   B Sure. _____ ?
   A No, that's all, thanks.
   B OK. That's _____ .

3. **A** _____ help me? I'm looking for this month's issue of *Vogue*. Can you tell me _____ ?
   B Right there on the middle rack. Next to *Latina*.
   A Thanks.
   B That's $3.50.

4. **A** Good morning. Can I have a _____ , please?
   B With sugar?
   A No, thanks. Oh, and a doughnut, please.
   B _____ there aren't _____ . We have some delicious muffins.
   A I'll have a blueberry muffin.
   B Will _____ today?
   A That's it.
   B _____ , please.
   A OK.

EVERYDAY ENGLISH
Prices and shopping

1 Practice the way we write and say prices in US currency.

American English		British English	
Written	**Spoken**	**Written**	**Spoken**
$1.00	a dollar	£1	a pound
50¢	fifty cents	50p	fifty p
$1.99	a dollar ninety-nine	£1.99	one pound ninety-nine
$16.40	sixteen-forty/sixteen dollars and forty cents	£16.40	sixteen pounds forty

T 4.6 Listen to the conversations and write the prices you hear.

1. __$6.00__ 2. _____ 3. _____ 4. _____ 5. _____ 6. _____

2 What's the current exchange rate between US dollars and your currency?

There are about five ... to the dollar.

In your country, how much is ... ?

- a pair of jeans
- a CD
- a hamburger
- a liter of gas

3 Make conversations in these places with a partner.
You can use the ideas to help you.

3. in a cafe

a black/light coffee
an espresso/a cappuccino
a pot of tea
a fruit juice
a bottle of mineral water
a piece of chocolate cake

1. in a clothing store

a shirt/tie
What size are you?
Small/medium/large
too small/too big/just
   right
No, thanks./I'll take it.

2. in a post office

some stamps
First class or express mail?
a letter/postcard to ...
send this package to ...
by air/by surface mail

4. in a drugstore

I have a stomachache/
   sore throat
conditioner
shaving cream
deodorant

5 What do you want to do?

Verb patterns 1 · Future forms · Hot verbs · How do you feel?

STARTER

Complete these sentences with ideas about you.

- Someday I want to ...
- I can ... but I can't ...
- Right now, I'd like to ...
- Tonight I'm going to ...
- I enjoy ... because I like ...

HOPES AND AMBITIONS
Verb patterns 1

1 Take a guess. Who do you think said each line below? Match the people with their hopes and ambitions.

1. ___ "I'd like to have my own business, something like a flying school."
2. ___ "I'm going to be an astronaut and fly to Mars."
3. ___ "I'm looking forward to having more time to do the things I want to do."
4. ___ "I would love to have one of my plays performed on Broadway."
5. ___ "We hope to find work as we go around the world."
6. ___ "We're thinking of moving, because the kids will be leaving home soon."

T 5.1 Listen and check.

2 Complete the chart.

	Ambitions/Plans	Reasons
Duane		
Maria		
Jim		
Martin		
Amy		
Helen		

3 <u>Underline</u> the examples of verb + verb in Exercise 1.

I'd like to have my own business.

Look at the tapescript on page 130. Find more examples of verb + verb.

a Duane, 9

c Jim, 29

d Martin, 39

e Amy, 49

GRAMMAR SPOT

1 Complete the sentences with the words *go abroad*. Put the verb *go* in the correct form.

> I want **to go abroad.**
> I'd like ...
> I can't ...
> I'm looking forward to ...
> I hope ...
> I enjoy ...
> I'm thinking of ...
> I'd love ...

2 What's the difference between these sentences?

> I like going to the movies.
> I'd like to go to the movies tonight.

▶▶ **Grammar Reference 5.1 and 5.2 p. 144**

Maria, 19 **b**

Helen, 59 **f**

Discussing grammar

1 In these sentences, one or two verbs are correct, but not all three. Put a check (✔) next to the correct verbs.

1. I _____ to write poetry.
   a. ✔ want   b. ☐ enjoy   c. ✔ 'd like

2. We _____ going to Hawaii for our vacation.
   a. ☐ are hoping   b. ☐ 're thinking of   c. ☐ like

3. I _____ go home early tonight.
   a. ☐ want   b. ☐ like   c. ☐ can

4. I _____ to see you again soon.
   a. ☐ hope   b. ☐ 'd like   c. ☐ 'm looking forward

5. Do you _____ learning English?
   a. ☐ want   b. ☐ enjoy   c. ☐ like

6. We _____ taking a few days off soon.
   a. ☐ 're thinking of   b. ☐ 'd love to   c. ☐ 're looking forward to

Make correct sentences with the other verbs.

I enjoy writing poetry.

Making questions

2 Complete the questions.

1. **A** I hope to go to college.
   B (What/want/study?) **What do you want to study?**

2. **A** One of my favorite hobbies is cooking.
   B (What/like/make?) _____

3. **A** I get terrible headaches.
   B (When/start/get/them?) _____

4. **A** We're planning our vacation now.
   B (Where/think of/go?) _____

5. **A** I'm tired.
   B (What/like/do/tonight?) _____

T 5.2 Listen and check. What are **A**'s answers? Practice the conversations with a partner.

Talking about you

3 Ask and answer the questions with a partner.

- What do you like doing on vacation?
- Where would you like to be right now?
- Do you like learning English?
- Would you like to take a break now?

4 Ask and answer questions about your future plans and ambitions.

Which countries ... go to?

How many children ...?

What ... after this course?

FUTURE INTENTIONS
going to and *will*

1 Match the pictures and sentences.

1. ☐ They're going to watch a baseball game.
2. ☐ I'll pick it up for you.
3. ☐ She's going to travel around the world.
4. ☐ Oh! I'll answer it.
5. ☐ Don't worry. I'll lend you some.
6. ☐ We're going out for dinner.

2 Add a line before and after the sentences in Exercise 1.

Before

I don't have any money.
What's Sue doing next year?
The phone's ringing.
Darn it! I dropped one.
What are you and Pete doing tonight?
What are the guys doing this afternoon?

After

Thank you. That's very nice of you.
I'm expecting a call.
Thanks. I'll pay you back tomorrow. I won't forget.
Lucky her!
The Chicago Cubs are playing.
It's my birthday.

T 5.3 Listen and check. Practice the conversations with a partner.

> **GRAMMAR SPOT**
>
> **1** Notice the forms of *will*.
>   **I'll** = short form
>   **I won't** = negative
> **2** All the sentences in Exercise 1 express intentions.
>   • Three intentions are spontaneous (= made at the moment of speaking). Which are they?
>   • Three intentions are premeditated (= made before the moment of speaking). What happened **before** each one?
>
> ▶▶ **Grammar Reference 5.3 p. 144**

PRACTICE

Let's have a party!

1 Your class has decided to have a party. Everyone has to help. Say at least five things you'll do.

> *I'll bring the music.*

> *I'll buy some potato chips.*

2 Your teacher didn't hear what you said. Listen to your teacher and correct him/her.

Teacher	**You**

> *I'll bring some music.*

> *No, **I'm** going to bring some music!*

> *Oh, all right. Well, I'll buy some potato chips.*

> *No, **I'm** going to buy some potato chips!*

Discussing grammar

3 Choose the correct verb form.

1. "My bag is so heavy."
   "Give it to me. *I'll carry* / *I'm going to carry* it for you."
2. I bought some warm boots because *I'll go* / *I'm going* skiing.
3. "Tony's back from vacation."
   "He is? *I'll give* / *I'm going to give* him a call."
4. "What are you doing tonight?"
   "*We'll see* / *We're going to see* a play at the theater."
5. "Are you coming to our class party?"
   "Yes, *I'll see* / *I'm going to see* you there."
6. Congratulations! I hear *you'll get married* / *you're going to get married*.
7. "I need to mail these letters."
   I'll mail / *I'm going to mail* them for you."
8. "Where are you going on your vacation this year?"
   "*We will go to* / *We're going to* Hawaii."

4 **T 5.4** Close your books. Listen to the beginnings of the conversations from Exercise 3 and complete them.

Check it

5 Correct the sentences.

1. What you want drink?
2. I have a soda, please.
3. I can't to help you.
4. It's starting rain.
5. I'm looking forward to see you again soon.
6. I think to change my job soon.
7. Call me tonight. I give you my phone number.
8. I go have a big party for my next birthday.

Talking about you

6 Talk to a partner about your plans for tonight, tomorrow, next weekend, your next vacation, New Year's …

> *What are you doing tonight / going to do tonight?*

> *I'm going to stay home and …*

> *Where are you going … ?*

> *I'm going to see …*

> *I think I'll …*

READING
Hollywood kids

1 What are some of the problems of being a teenager? Put a check (✓) in the boxes on the left.

☐ drugs	☐
☐ violence in the streets	☐
☐ they don't have enough money	☐
☐ their parents don't give them enough attention	☐
☐ they worry about how they look	☐
☐ they have no interests or ambitions	☐
☐ their parents want them to do well in life	☐
☐ they're too old to be children, but too young to be adults	☐

2 Read the text about Hollywood kids. What are some of their problems? Put a check (✓) in the boxes on the right. Are there any differences?

3 Are these sentences true (✓) or false (✗)? Correct the false sentences.

1. Everyone in Hollywood is rich and famous.
2. Hollywood kids don't lead ordinary lives.
3. They understand the value of what they have.
4. Trent Maguire is ambitious.
5. The adults try hard to be good parents.
6. Amanda's mother listens to all her daughter's problems.
7. The kids are often home alone.
8. Their parents organize every part of their lives.
9. The kids don't want to be children.
10. All the kids complain about living in Hollywood.

4 Answer the questions.

1. In what way do Rachel, Lindsey, and Trent live unreal lives?
2. Does anything surprise you about what the kids say?
3. What are their ambitions?

What do you think?

- Do you feel sorry for children in Hollywood? Is there anything about their lives that you would like?
- What is your opinion of their parents?
- Do teenagers around the world think the same as Hollywood kids?
- Do you think it is dangerous to have everything you want?

Hollywood
What's it like

In Hollywood, the home of the entertainment industry, it seems like everybody wants to be rich, famous, and beautiful. Nobody wants to be old, unknown, or poor. For kids growing up in such a world, life can be difficult. Their parents are ambitious, and the children are part of the parents' ambitions.

Parents pay for extravagant parties, expensive cars, and designer clothes. The children have everything, but never learn the value of anything because it all comes so easy. A 13-year-old boy, Trent Maguire, has a driver, credit cards, and unlimited cash to do what he wants when he wants. "Someday, I'll make more than my Dad," he boasts.

Parents buy care and attention for their children because they have no time to give it themselves. Amanda's mother employs a bodyguard/chauffeur, a personal trainer, a nutritionist, a singing coach, and a counselor to take care of all of her 15-year-old daughter's needs.

Often there is no parent at home most days, so children decide whether to make their own meals or go out to restaurants, when to watch television or do homework. They organize their own social lives. There's no place for childhood games. Children become adults before they're ready.

Hollywood has always been a place where dreams come true. Lots of Hollywood kids live in a world where money, beauty, and pleasure are the only gods. Will children around the world soon start to think the same? Or do they already?

〞Looks are very important in Hollywood. If you're good-looking, you'll go far. I want to be a beautician. You grow up really fast here. Everyone is in a rush to be an adult, to be going to clubs. It's not cool to be a kid.〝 **Melissa, age 18** ▼

kids

By Lonnie Feldman

when you have it all?

"I live in a hotel and when I come home from school, there are maybe 80 people who say 'Good day' to me. It's their job to say that. In the bathroom there are mirrors everywhere. I love looking at myself. I can spend five hours doing my hair and posing. I'm going to be a model."
Rachel, age 10 ▶

▲ "I've wanted to get my nose done since I was 12. My friends started having plastic surgery and liposuction during my freshman year of high school. My nose cost $10,000. But it was worth it. It changed my life. I'm gonna get into the movies."
Lindsey, age 18

VOCABULARY
Hot verbs—*have, go, come*

1 The verbs *have, go,* and *come* are very common in English. Look at these examples from the text on pages 38–39.

have	go	come
... they have no time ... The children have everything ...	You'll go far. ... going to clubs.	... it all comes so easy. ... a place where dreams come true.

2 Put *have, go,* or *come* into each blank.

__have__ an accident   _____ a cold

_____ in first in a race   _____ wrong

_____ out for a meal   _____ a meeting

_____ and see me   _____ abroad

_____ shopping

3 Fill in the blanks with the correct form of *have, go,* or *come.*

1. We're __having__ a party next Saturday. Would you like _____ ?

2. I _____ a terrible headache. Can I _____ home, please?

3. You must see my new apartment. _____ over and _____ a drink sometime.

4. "I'm _____ out now, Mom. Bye!" "OK. _____ a good time. What time are you _____ home?"

5. Hi, Dave. Pete _____ breakfast right now. I'll _____ and tell him you're here.

6. _____ on! Get out of bed. It's time _____ to school.

7. It's a beautiful day. Let's _____ to the park. We can _____ a picnic.

8. I'm _____ skiing next week. Do you _____ any ski clothes I could borrow?

LISTENING
You've got a friend

1 Who says these things? Write *1, 2,* or *3.*

1. Your best friend
2. Your boyfriend/girlfriend
3. Your ex-boyfriend/ex-girlfriend

_____ I'll love you forever.

_____ I'll never forget you.

_____ I'll always be there for you.

_____ I'll always remember the times we had together.

_____ I'll do anything for you.

_____ You'll never find anyone who loves you more than I do.

2 Listen to the first verse of the song. Discuss these questions.

1. Do you think the man and woman live together?
2. Is it a close relationship?
3. What is the relationship between them now? What do you think it was in the past?

3 **T 5.5** Listen and complete the song.

You've Got a Friend, by Carole King

When you're down and troubled
And you need a _____
And nothing, but _____
Close your eyes and think of me
And soon I _____
To brighten up even your darkest nights.
(Chorus)
You just call out my name,
and you know wherever I am
I _____ to see you again.
Winter, spring, _____
All you have to do is call
And I'll be there, yeah, yeah, yeah,
You've got a friend.
If the sky above you
_____ and full of clouds
And that old north _____
Keep your head together
And _____
And soon I'll be knocking on your door.
Hey, _____ that you've got a friend?
People can be so cold.
_____ and desert you.
Well they'll take your soul if you let them.
Oh, yeah, but _____ .
(Chorus)

EVERYDAY ENGLISH
How do you feel?

1 Look at the photos. How do the people feel?

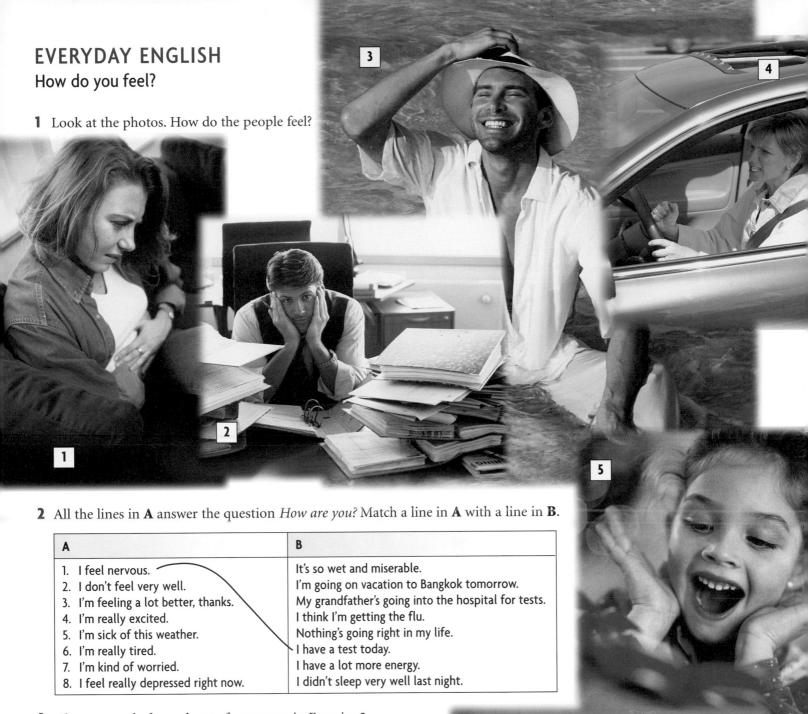

2 All the lines in **A** answer the question *How are you?* Match a line in **A** with a line in **B**.

A	B
1. I feel nervous.	It's so wet and miserable.
2. I don't feel very well.	I'm going on vacation to Bangkok tomorrow.
3. I'm feeling a lot better, thanks.	My grandfather's going into the hospital for tests.
4. I'm really excited.	I think I'm getting the flu.
5. I'm sick of this weather.	Nothing's going right in my life.
6. I'm really tired.	I have a test today.
7. I'm kind of worried.	I have a lot more energy.
8. I feel really depressed right now.	I didn't sleep very well last night.

3 Choose a reply for each set of sentences in Exercise 2.

____ a. Cheer up! Things can't be that bad!
____ b. Why don't you go home and go to bed?
____ c. I'm sorry to hear that, but I'm sure he'll be all right.
____ d. I know. We really need some sun.
____ e. That happens to me sometimes. I just read in bed.
_1_ f. Good luck! Do your best.
____ g. That's good. I'm glad to hear it.
____ h. That's great. Have a good time.

T 5.6 Listen and compare your answers.

4 Make more conversations with a partner about these things:

- a wedding
- a visit to the dentist
- problems with parents or teenage children
- a letter from the bank
- a big project at work or school
- an argument with a boyfriend/girlfriend

6 The best in the world

STARTER

1 What is the capital city of your country? What is the population? Is it an old or modern city?

2 Write down two things that you like about your capital and two things that you don't like.

> *I like traveling on the subway in Washington, D.C., but I don't like the buses. They're too slow.*

WORLD TRAVEL
What's it like?

1 Read about Todd Bridges.

2 What do you know about the three cities in the chart below? Where are they?

3 **T 6.1** Listen to what Todd says about Melbourne, Dubai, and Paris. Write the adjectives he uses for each city. Compare with a partner.

Melbourne	Dubai	Paris
big beautiful		

GRAMMAR SPOT

1 Match the questions and answers.

	It's beautiful.
Do you like Paris?	Yes, I do.
What's Paris like?	It has lots of old buildings.
	No, I don't.

2 Which question in 1 means: *Tell me about Paris.*

▶▶ **Grammar Reference 6.1 p. 145**

4 Work with a partner. Ask and answer questions about the places Todd visited.

> *What's Melbourne like?*

> *It's ...*   *It has ...*   *There are ...*

TODD BRIDGES

Todd Bridges is only 17 years old, but he is already a successful tennis player. He comes from Chicago, but he travels all over the world playing tennis. Last year he played in tennis championships in Melbourne, Dubai, and Paris.

PRACTICE

What's Chicago like?

1 You are asking Todd about Chicago. Complete the questions with *is* or *are* and the correct words from the box.

| the restaurants | the people | the weather |
| the nightlife | the buildings | |

1. **You** What _'s the weather_ like?
   Todd Well, Chicago's called "the windy city," and it really can be windy!
2. **You** What _____ like?
   Todd They're very interesting. You meet people from all over the world.
3. **You** What _____ like?
   Todd A lot of them are very, very tall. The Sears Tower is 110 stories high.
4. **You** What _____ like?
   Todd They're very good. You can find food from every country in the world.
5. **You** What _____ like?
   Todd Oh, it's wonderful. There's lots to do in Chicago.

2 **T 6.2** Listen and check. Practice with a partner.

3 Ask and answer the same questions about the town or city you are in now.

BIG, BIGGER, BIGGEST!
Comparatives and superlatives

1 Read the second part of the conversation with Todd. He compares the places he visited last year. Can you complete any of the sentences?

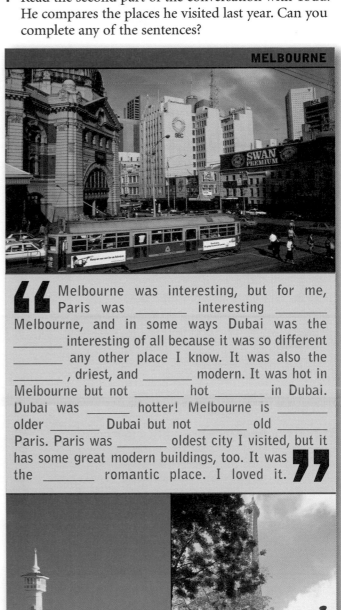

MELBOURNE

" Melbourne was interesting, but for me, Paris was _____ interesting _____ Melbourne, and in some ways Dubai was the _____ interesting of all because it was so different _____ any other place I know. It was also the _____, driest, and _____ modern. It was hot in Melbourne but not _____ hot _____ in Dubai. Dubai was _____ hotter! Melbourne is _____ older _____ Dubai but not _____ old _____ Paris. Paris was _____ oldest city I visited, but it has some great modern buildings, too. It was the _____ romantic place. I loved it. "

DUBAI   PARIS

T 6.3 Listen and check.

1 What are the comparative and superlative forms of the following adjectives? What are the rules?

   a. small   c. busy
      cold   noisy
      near   dry

   b. big   d. beautiful
      hot   interesting
      wet   exciting

2 These adjectives are irregular. What are the comparative and superlative forms?

   | far   good   bad |

3 Adjectives also combine with *as ... as*.
   Dubai isn't **as** cosmopolitan **as** Chicago.

▶▶ **Grammar Reference 6.2 p. 145**

2 **T 6.4** Listen and repeat the sentences.

   /hɑtər ðən/
This summer's hotter than last.

   /əz hɑt əz/
It wasn't as hot as this last year.

3 Practice these sentences with a partner.

   It isn't as warm today as it was yesterday.
   But it's warmer than it was last week.
   I'm not as tall as you, but I'm taller than Ana.
   My car's more expensive than John's.
   But it isn't as expensive as Ana's.

T 6.5 Listen and check.

4 Learn this poem by heart.

   Good, better, best.
   Never, never rest
   'til your good is better,
   And your better best.

PRACTICE

Comparing four capital cities

1 Match the cities and the photographs. Of which countries are these the capital cities?

| Washington, D.C.   Tokyo   Stockholm   Brasilia |

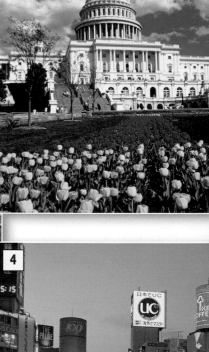

2 Work with a partner.

   Student A Go to page 119 and read about Tokyo and Washington, D.C.
   Student B Go to page 121 and read about Stockholm and Brasilia.

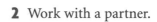

Conversations

3 Work with a partner and continue these conversations.

1. **A** I moved to a new apartment last week.
   B Really? What's it like?
   A Well, it's _bigger_ than my old one but it isn't as modern, and …

2. **A** I hear Sandy and Al broke up.
   B Yeah. Sandy has a new boyfriend.
   A Really? What's he like?
   B Well, he's _____ than Al, and …

3. **A** We have a new teacher.
   B Really? What's she like?
   A Well, I think she's the _____ teacher we've ever had …

4. **A** Did you get a new car?
   B Well, it's secondhand, but it's new to me.
   A What's it like?
   B Well, it's _____ than my old car …

Act out a conversation for the class. Whose conversation is the longest?

T 6.6 Listen and compare. Repeat the last lines.

Check it

4 Correct the sentences.

1. He's more older than he looks.
2. Laura's as tall than her mother.
3. "What does Las Vegas like?" "It's really exciting!"
4. Trains in Tokyo are more crowded that in Washington, D.C.
5. Harvard is one of oldest universities in North America.
6. This is more hard than I expected.
7. Who is the most rich person in the world?
8. Everything is more cheap in my country.

LISTENING AND SPEAKING
Living in another country

1 What do you know about Sweden? What is the country like? What are the people like? Discuss these statements about Sweden. Do you think they are true (✓) or false (✗)?

1. In winter there is only one hour of daylight.
2. Swedish people look forward to winter.
3. The houses are cold in winter.
4. In Sweden, it gets much hotter in summer than in New York or Washington, D.C.
5. In parts of Sweden the sun never sets from May to July.
6. Many people in the United States work longer hours than people in Sweden.
7. Swedes always start work early in the morning.
8. Country cottages in Sweden are usually very luxurious.
9. All houses have a sauna.
10. The whole family likes to sit in the sauna together.

2 **T 6.7** You are going to listen to Jane talking to her friend about her life in Sweden. Jane comes from the United States, but three years ago she married a Swede and went to live and work in Stockholm. Listen and check your answers to Exercise 1.

3 Compare your country with what you learn about Sweden.

In my country it gets dark at five o'clock in winter, and it's much warmer than in Sweden.

READING AND SPEAKING
A tale of two millionaires

1 Who are the richest people in your country? Where does their money come from? How do they spend their money?

2 Match the verbs and nouns. Many of them have to do with money.

Verbs	Nouns
1. make	a bank account
2. spoil	poverty
3. wear	a thief
4. open	a will
5. live in	stocks and bonds
6. inherit	a child
7. buy	a leg
8. arrest	ragged clothes
9. invest	a lot of money from someone
10. amputate	a lot of money in something

3 You are going to read about two millionaires. One was very stingy, the other very generous. First read *quickly* about Milton Petrie. Can you remember any examples of his kindness?

4 Now read *quickly* about Hetty Green. Can you remember any examples of her stinginess?

5 Work with a partner.

Student A Read about Milton Petrie.
Student B Read about Hetty Green.

Answer the questions with your partner.

1. When were Milton and Hetty born?
2. What were their parents like?
3. How did Milton and Hetty become so wealthy?
4. Who wore ragged clothes?
5. What was the stingiest thing Hetty did?
6. Why did Milton like making a lot of money?
7. Who did they marry?
8. When did they die? How old were they?
9. Who left the most money? Who did they leave it to?

What do you think?

Discuss these questions in small groups.

- How were Milton and Hetty's childhoods different?
- How did their childhoods affect them later?
- Why was Milton especially generous to police officers?
- Why did Hetty's daughter build a hospital?
- What was the kindest thing Milton did?
- Who had the happier life? Milton or Hetty?

A tale of
Some millionaires

Milton Petrie

The Most Generous Man in the World

Every morning, billionaire Milton Petrie walked from his New York apartment and bought a newspaper from the ragged old man on the street corner. One morning the man wasn't there. Petrie learned that he was very ill in the city hospital. Immediately he paid his hospital bill and later, when the man died, paid for his funeral.

Milton with the model he helped

two millionaires

spend it and some save it. **Elizabeth Wilson** reports on one of each.

The old man was just one of many people that Milton Petrie helped with his money. Whenever he read about personal disasters in the newspaper, Petrie sent generous checks, especially to the families of police officers or fire fighters injured at work. He also sent checks to a mother who lost five children in a fire, and a beautiful model, whose face was cut in a knife attack. It cost him millions of dollars, but he still had millions left. He said that he was lucky in business and he wanted to help those less fortunate than himself. "The nice thing is, the harder I work, the more money I make, and the more people I can help."

Milton Petrie died in 1994, when he was 92. His will was 120 pages long because he left $150 million to 383 people. His widow, Carroll, his fourth and last wife, said his generosity was a result of the poverty of his early years. His family was poor but kindhearted. His father was a Russian immigrant who became a police officer, but he never arrested anyone; he was too kind. He couldn't even give out a parking ticket.

Hetty Green

The Richest, Stingiest Woman in the World

Henrietta (Hetty) Green was a very spoiled, only child. She was born in Massachusetts in 1835. Her father was a millionaire businessman. Her mother was often ill, and so from the age of two her father took her with him to work and taught her about stocks and bonds. At the age of six she started reading the daily financial newspapers and she opened her own bank account.

Her father died when she was 21, and she inherited $7.5 million. She went to New York and invested on Wall Street. Hetty saved every penny, eating in the cheapest restaurants for 15 cents. She became one of the richest and most hated women in the world. She was called "The Witch of Wall Street." At 33 she married Edward Green, a multi-millionaire, and had two children, Ned and Sylvia.

Hetty's stinginess was legendary. She always argued about prices in stores. She walked to the local grocery store to buy broken cookies that were much cheaper, and to get a free bone for her much loved dog, Dewey. Once she lost a two-cent stamp and spent the whole night looking for it. She never bought clothes and always wore the same long, ragged black skirt. Worst of all, when her son, Ned, fell and injured his knee, she refused to pay for a doctor and spent hours looking for free medical help. In the end Ned's leg was amputated.

When she died in 1916 she left her children $100 million (worth $9.3 billion today). Her daughter built a hospital with her money.

VOCABULARY AND PRONUNCIATION

Synonyms

1 We often use synonyms in conversation because we don't want to repeat words.

*It's a **beautiful** day today!*

*Yes, it's really **nice** out.*

Complete the conversations using an adjective of similar meaning from the box.

> sick of   generous   great   enormous   modern   wealthy

1. **A** "Mary's family is very rich."
   B "Well, I knew her uncle was very ___wealthy___."
2. **A** "Look at all these new buildings!"
   B "Yes. This city's much more _____ than I expected."
3. **A** "Wasn't that movie wonderful?"
   B "Yes, it was _____."
4. **A** "George doesn't have much money, but he's so thoughtful."
   B "Yes, he is. He's one of the most _____ people I know."
5. **A** "Steve and Elaine's house is huge."
   B "Yes, it's absolutely _____."
6. **A** "I'm bored with this lesson!"
   B "I know, I'm really _____ it, too!"

2 **T 6.8** Listen and check. Listen again, paying particular attention to the stress and intonation. Practice the conversations with a partner.

Antonyms

3 We can also use antonyms in conversation to avoid repeating words.

*What an **awful** meal!*

*I know. It wasn't very **good**, was it?*

Match the following adjectives with their *two* opposites in Exercise 1.

interested	*bored*	*sick of*
awful	_____	_____
stingy	_____	_____
old	_____	_____
poor	_____	_____
tiny	_____	_____

4 Sometimes it is more polite to use *not very* and an opposite adjective.

Tom is short.	Tom **isn't very** tall.
His clothes are dirty.	His clothes **aren't very** clean.

Restate these sentences using *not very*.

1. Mark's apartment is tiny.
2. Paul and Sue are stingy.
3. This TV show is boring.
4. Their children are rude.
5. John looks miserable.
6. His sister is stupid.

5 **T 6.9** Listen and check. Pay particular attention to the stress and intonation. Practice with your partner.

EVERYDAY ENGLISH
Directions

1 Look at the map of Pleasantville and find these things:
- a park
- woods
- a pond
- a path
- a hill
- a bridge
- a gate

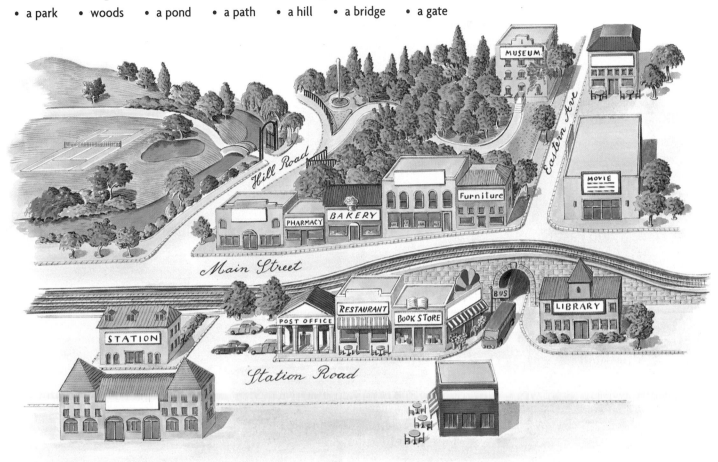

2 Read these descriptions and add the places to the map.

coffee shop (x2)	hotel	bank
supermarket	flower shop	

1. The hotel is on Station Road, across from the train station.
2. The bank is on the corner of Main Street and Hill Road. It is next to the pharmacy.
3. The supermarket is between the bakery and the furniture store.
4. There is a bus stop in front of the flower shop.
5. There are two coffee shops. The Big Jolt is on Eastern Avenue, behind the movie theater, and the Java is on Station Road, across from the flower shop.

3 Ask and answer questions with a partner about the other places. Use the prepositions from Exercise 2.

Where's the library?

It's on the corner of Station Road and Eastern Avenue, across from the flower shop.

4 Complete the directions from the tennis court to the museum with the prepositions in the box. Look at the map to help you.

past	up	down	over	into (x2)	out of	across	through (x2)

You go __down__ the path, _____ the pond, _____ the bridge, and _____ the gate. Then you go _____ the road. Take the path _____ the park and _____ the woods. When you come _____ the woods, just follow the path _____ the steps and _____ the museum. It takes about five minutes or less.

T 6.10 Listen and check.

5 Give your partner directions to get to your home from your school.

7 Fame

Present Perfect · *for*, *since* · Adverbs, word pairs · Short answers

STARTER ▶ What is the Past Simple and the past participle of these verbs?

sing   be   sell   win   have   hear   do   eat   know   break

FAMOUS SINGERS
Present Perfect and Past Simple

1 Look at the photographs of two well-known American singers. How do you think they are related?

Complete the sentences with *He* or *She*.

1. __He__ sang pop music and jazz. __She__ sings jazz, pop, and rhythm & blues.
2. _____ recorded more than 600 songs and sold over 50 million records. _____ has made over 17 albums so far.
3. _____ was born in Los Angeles and has lived in California for most of her life. _____ was born in Montgomery, Alabama, grew up in Chicago, then later moved to California.
4. _____ has been married twice and has one son. _____ married for the first time in 1976. _____ was married twice and had five children.

T 7.1 Listen and check.

> **GRAMMAR SPOT**
>
> **1** Find examples of the Past Simple in the four sentences above.
> Find examples of the Present Perfect.
>
> **2** Complete the rule.
> We make the Present Perfect with the auxiliary verb _____ + the _____.
>
> **3** Why are different tenses used in these sentences?
> Nat King Cole **recorded** more than 600 songs.
> Natalie Cole **has recorded** 17 albums.
>
> ▶▶ **Grammar Reference 7.1 and 7.2 p. 146**

Nat King Cole (1919–1965)

2 Put the verbs in the Present Perfect or Past Simple.

1. Nat King Cole __won__ (win) many awards, including a Grammy Award in 1959 and Capitol Records' "Tower of Achievement" award. Natalie Cole _____ (win) eight Grammies and many other awards for her singing.

2. He _____ (have) his own TV show in 1956 and _____ (appear) in a number of movies. She _____ (appear) in several TV specials and TV movies.

3. She _____ (receive) a degree in psychology from the University of Massachusetts in 1972. She _____ (live) mostly in California since then.

4. She _____ (be) a recording artist for more than 25 years. She _____ (record) her first album, *Inseparable,* in 1975. With that album she _____ (win) two Grammy Awards in 1976.

5. Her remarkable album, *Unforgettable with Love,* _____ (come) out in 1991. On it, she sang the song "Unforgettable" as a "duet" with her father's voice. Since then, the album _____ (sell) over five million copies.

T 7.2 Listen and check.

Natalie Cole (1950–)

3 Here are the answers to some questions about Natalie Cole. What are the questions?

1. Over 17. (*How many … ?*)
How many albums has she made?
2. In California. (*Where … for most of her life?*)
3. Twice. (*How many times … ?*)
4. One, a son. (*How many … ?*)
5. Yes, she has. She's won eight Grammies. (*… awards for her singing?*)
6. The University of Massachusetts. (*What university … ?*)
7. For more than 25 years. (*How long … ?*)
8. In 1975. (*When … ?*)

T 7.3 Listen and check.

PRACTICE

Discussing grammar

1 Choose the correct verb form.
1. *Have you ever been* / *Did you ever go* to a rock concert?
2. I *saw* / *have seen* The Flash last week.
3. I love rock and roll. I *like* / *have liked* it all my life.
4. The Flash's concert *was* / *has been* fantastic.
5. I *have bought* / *bought* all their albums since then.
6. The Flash *have been* / *are* together since the early 1990s.

Find someone who …

2 Choose a number and circle it.

1	2	3	4	5
6	7	8	9	10
11	12	13	14	15
16	17	18	19	20

Now turn to page 122 and match your number to one of the sentences, which begin *Find someone who … .*

for and *since*

4 Complete the time expressions with *for* or *since*.

1. <u> for </u> a year
2. _____ half an hour
3. _____ August
4. _____ nine o'clock
5. _____ I was a kid
6. _____ a couple of days
7. _____ months
8. _____ 1999

5 Match a line in **A** and **B** and a sentence in **C**. There is more than one answer!

A	B	C
1. I've known my best friend	from 1994 to 2000.	It's OK. I kind of like it.
2. I last went to a movie	for an hour.	I went camping with some friends.
3. I've had this watch	two weeks ago.	We met when we were ten.
4. We've used this book	since 1989.	I really need a cup of coffee.
5. We lived in our old apartment	since the beginning of the semester.	My dad gave it to me for my birthday.
6. We haven't had a break	for years.	We moved because we needed a bigger place.
7. I last took a vacation	for three years.	It had Tom Cruise in it.
8. This building has been a school	in 1999.	Before that it was an office building.

T 7.4 Listen and check. Make similar sentences about you.

Asking questions

6 Complete the conversation.
What tenses are the three questions?

A Where _____ live, Mi-Young?

B In an apartment near the park.

A How long _____ there?

B For three years.

A And why _____ move?

B We wanted to live in a nicer area.

T 7.5 Listen and check. Practice the conversation with a partner.

7 Make more conversations, using the same tenses.

1. **A** What ... do?	2. **A** ... have a car?	3. **A** ... know Pete Brown?
B I work ...	**B** Yes, I ...	**B** Yes, I ...
A How long ... ?	**A** How long ... ?	**A** How long ... ?
B For ...	**B** Since ...	**B** For ...
A What ... do before that?	**A** How much ... pay for it?	**A** Where ... meet him?
B I worked ...	**B** It was ...	**B** We ...

8 With a partner, ask and answer questions beginning *How long ... ?*

> *How long have you lived / worked / known / had ... ?*

Then get some more information.

> *Why did you move?*

> *What did you do before ... ?*

> *Where did you meet ... ?*

LISTENING AND SPEAKING
The band Style

1 What kind of music do you like? Who are your favorite bands and singers? If you could meet your favorite band or singer, what would you ask them?

2 **T 7.6** Listen to an interview with two musicians, Suzie and Gary, from the band Style. Put **S** or **G** in Columns 1 and 2. Put ✓ or ✗ in Column 3.

1. **What do they do in the band?**	2. **Who have they played with?**	3. **Where have they visited?**
☐ guitar	☐ UB40	☐ Mexico
☐ keyboards	☐ Britney Spears	☐ Japan
☐ drums	☐ Phil Collins	☐ the UK
☐ harmonica	☐ Genesis	☐ Brazil
☐ vocalist	☐ Ricky Martin	☐ Taiwan
	☐ Bon Jovi	☐ Australia
	☐ Ace	☐ France

Which bands have they played with? Which countries have they been to?

3 Answer the questions.
1. Why do Suzie and Gary feel tired?
2. What have they done this year?
3. Have they had a good time?
4. What was special about the song "Mean Street"?
5. How many years have they been together?
6. Where do they want to go?
7. What jobs has Gary had?
   What about Suzie? (*She's worked …)*

Language work

4 Make sentences about Suzie and Gary with the phrases in the boxes.

A	B
in April	since 1997
in 1995	about 25
two years ago	15 years
when she got out of college	since he was 17

What tense are the verbs in the sentences from **A**? What about **B**?

5 Ask and answer the questions.
- What/do/before forming Style?
- … be/to South America?
- How/meet each other?
- How many recordings/make?

Role play

6 Work in groups of four.

Student A and **Student B**   You are members of a band.

Student C and **Student D**   You are are journalists who are going to interview the band.

Ask and answer questions about:
- the name of the band
- what kind of music the band plays
- who plays what instrument
- what has influenced their music
- how long they have been together
- the records they have made
- the places they have visited

READING
Celebrity interview

1 Which celebrities are in the news right now? Why are they in the news? What have they done?

2 Look at the article from *Hi! Magazine*. Who is the couple in the interview? Are there magazines like this in your country? What kind of stories do they have?

3 Read the article quickly and put these questions in the right place.

1. Have there ever been times when you have thought "This relationship isn't working"?
2. Terry, many professional athletes are tough, but you seem very sensitive. Why is this?
3. You're both extremely busy in your separate careers. How do you find time to be together?
4. How did you two meet?
5. What's it like to be superstars?

4 Read the article again and answer the questions.

1. Why are they famous?
2. They are both successful in their careers. What have they done?
3. In what ways are they normal people? What is not normal about their lives?
4. How do you know they're in love?
5. Was it love at first sight?
6. What is their attitude to newspapers and "other people"?
7. Why do some people want them to split up?
8. In what way is Terry unusual for a professional athlete?

5 Work in groups of three. Read the text aloud.

Language work

6 Choose the correct tense.

1. Donna and Terry *are / have been / were* together for two years.
2. They *like / have liked / liked* watching TV in the evenings.
3. They *meet / have met / met* after a baseball game.
4. They *have lived / live / lived* in their new home since April.
5. Terry *is / has been / was* in love just once.

Project

7 Buy a magazine like *Hi!*, and find an interview with a famous couple. Bring it to class and tell the class about it.

THE POP STAR AND THE BASEBALL PLAYER
DONNA FLYNN & TERRY WISEMAN
TALK TO *HI! MAGAZINE* ABOUT THEIR LOVE FOR EACH OTHER

This is the most famous couple in America. She is the pop star who has had ten number-one songs—more than any other single artist. He has hit at least 40 home runs every baseball season for the past 4 years and has played on the championship team in the World Series twice. Together they make about $40 million a year. They invited *Hi! Magazine* into their luxurious home.

?

Donna: A lot of the time since we've been together, one of us has been away. We really have to try hard to be together. We have both flown all over the world just to spend a few hours together.
Terry: Obviously, people say, "Oh, you have all this money, what are you going to spend it on?" But the best thing is that money buys us the freedom to be together.

?

Donna: It hasn't changed us. We are still the same people. Newspapers have told terrible stories about us, but it's all lies.
Terry: Our perfect evening is sitting in front of the TV with a pizza. Our favorite shows are *ER* and *Friends*. You won't find photos of us coming out of bars and clubs drunk, after spending the night with a whole load of famous people.

Donna says: "We are so totally in love. Right now, I'm the happiest I've ever been."

?

Donna: I went to one of his games because I liked him and I wanted to meet him. It's funny, because I'm not really interested in baseball, so when I met him after the game, I didn't know what to say to him.
Terry: I'm very shy. We just looked at each other from opposite sides of the room. But I said to my teammate, "She's the one for me. I'm going to marry her someday." Fortunately, she came to another game, and we started talking then.

?

Donna: Not really. Naturally, it's hard when you're away from each other, but in a way this has made us stronger.   ▷

Donna and Terry have been together for just over two years. They have lived in their new house since April. She says: "He has good taste —but not as good as mine!"

A lot of people would love to see us split up. People have accused Terry of things …

Terry: Of course you have to be ready to give and take in any relationship. There's a trust between us, and as long as that's there, our love will last.

?

Terry: The fact is that this is the first time I've been in love. I think that when you meet the person that you want to spend the rest of your life with, you give your whole life to that person. Nothing else matters.

Donna: We mean the world to each other. Neither of us will do anything to spoil it. **HI!**

Terry says: "She's the only woman I've ever loved."

VOCABULARY

Adverbs

1 Many adverbs end in *-ly*.

> slowly   carefully   usually

Find some more examples in the text on pages 54–55.

2 There are also many adverbs that don't end in *-ly*. Find these adverbs in the text.

> together   hard   still   just   of course

3 Complete the sentences with one of these adverbs.

> still
> nearly
> only
> of course
> together

1. "Do you love me?" __Of course__ I do. I'm crazy about you."
2. I called Tom at 10:00 in the morning, but he was _____ in bed.
3. It's our anniversary today. We've been _____ for 15 years.
4. Kate is very fussy about food. She _____ eats pasta and tortilla chips.
5. She was very ill and _____ died, but fortunately she got better.

4 Complete the sentences with one of these adverbs.

> at last   exactly   too   especially   just

1. I like all Russian novelists, __especially__ Tolstoy.
2. "I hate ironing." "Me, _____ . It's so boring."
3. "Are you telling me that we have no money?" "_____ . Not a penny."
4. I met her on December 30, _____ before New Year's.
5. _____ I have finished this exercise. Thank goodness. It was so boring.

Word pairs

1 There are many idiomatic expressions that consist of two words joined by *and*. Here is an example from the text on pages 54–55.

*"Of course you have to be ready to **give and take** in any relationship."*

2 Match the words.

A	B
ladies	and don'ts
sick	and then
now	and pepper
yes	and quiet
dos	and down
up	and tired
peace	and sound
safe	and gentlemen
salt	and no

> Good evening ...

3 Complete the sentences with one of the expressions in Exercise 2 above.

1. "Do you still play tennis?" "Not regularly. Just __now and then__ , when I have time."
2. This is a pretty relaxed place to work. There aren't many _____ .
3. Here you are at last! I've been so worried! Thank goodness you've arrived _____ .
4. "Do you like your new job?" "_____ . The money's OK, but I don't like my boss."
5. Sometimes there are too many people in the house. I go out on the patio for some _____ .
6. Good evening, _____ . It gives me great pleasure to talk to you all tonight.
7. "How's your grandmother?" "_____ . There are good days, and then not such good days."
8. It's been so wet! I'm _____ of this rain. When will it ever stop?

T 7.7 Listen and check.

EVERYDAY ENGLISH
Short answers

1 **T 7.8** Listen to the conversations. What's the difference between them? Which sounds more polite?

> **!** 1 When we answer Yes/No questions, we often repeat a subject and the auxiliary verb. Complete these short answers.
>
> Do you like cooking?   Yes, I _do_ .
> Is it raining?   No, it _____ .
> Have you been to Hawaii?   Yes, I _____ .
> Are you good at chess?   No, I _____ .
> Can you speak Spanish?   Yes, I _____ .
>
> 2 It also helps a conversation if you can add more information.
>
> Do you like cooking?   Yes, I do, as a matter of fact. I especially like Italian food.

2 Complete the short answers. Continue with a line from the speech bubbles below.

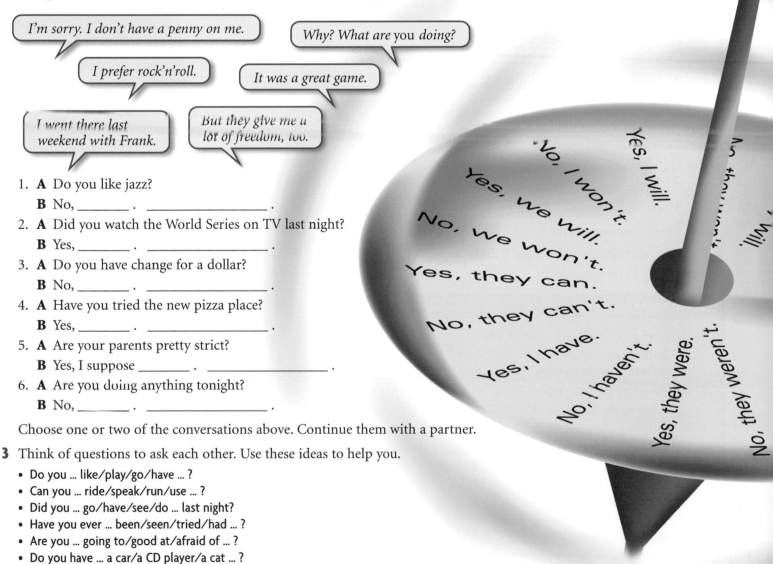

> *I'm sorry. I don't have a penny on me.*

> *Why? What are you doing?*

> *I prefer rock'n'roll.*

> *It was a great game.*

> *I went there last weekend with Frank.*

> *But they give me a lot of freedom, too.*

1. **A** Do you like jazz?
   B No, _____ . _____ .
2. **A** Did you watch the World Series on TV last night?
   B Yes, _____ . _____ .
3. **A** Do you have change for a dollar?
   B No, _____ . _____ .
4. **A** Have you tried the new pizza place?
   B Yes, _____ . _____ .
5. **A** Are your parents pretty strict?
   B Yes, I suppose _____ . _____ .
6. **A** Are you doing anything tonight?
   B No, _____ . _____ .

Choose one or two of the conversations above. Continue them with a partner.

3 Think of questions to ask each other. Use these ideas to help you.

- Do you ... like/play/go/have ... ?
- Can you ... ride/speak/run/use ... ?
- Did you ... go/have/see/do ... last night?
- Have you ever ... been/seen/tried/had ... ?
- Are you ... going to/good at/afraid of ... ?
- Do you have ... a car/a CD player/a cat ... ?

4 Stand up and ask your questions. Use short answers in your replies.

8 Dos and don'ts

have (got) to • should/must • Words that go together • A visit to the doctor

STARTER ▶ What's true for you? Make sentences about your life.

I have to ...   I don't have to ...
• get up early every morning   • pay bills   • go to school   • work on weekends   • do housework

WORK, WORK
have (got) to

1 **T 8.1** Listen to Steve talking about his job. What do you think his job is? Would you like his job? Why/Why not?

2 Complete Steve's sentences with the words from the box.

don't have to   have to   had to   do you have to   didn't have to

1. I _____ work very long hours.
2. _____ work on weekends?
3. I _____ wash the dishes.
4. We _____ learn the basics.
5. I _____ wait too long to get a job.

3 Change the sentences in Exercise 2 using *he*.

He has to work very long hours.

GRAMMAR SPOT

1 *Have* can express possession or an action.
I **have** my own apartment.
We **have** a test tomorrow.

2 *Have to* expresses obligation.
He **has to** work long hours. I**'ve got to** go now. Bye!

3 Write the question and negative with *have to*.
I have to get up early.
What time ____ you _____ get up?
I _____ get up early.
Put the sentence in the past.
Yesterday I _____ get up early.

▶▶ **Grammar Reference 8.1 p. 147**

4 What are some of the other things Steve has to do?

WHAT'S MY JOB?
STEVE BARNES

58   Unit 8 • Dos and don'ts

PRACTICE

Pronunciation

1 **T 8.2** Listen to these s~
pronunciations of '~

/hæv/

1. I have a good jo~

/hæz/

2. He has a nice car.

/hæd/   /hæt~

3. I had a good time.   I had t~

T 8.2 Listen again and repeat.

Jobs

2 Work with a partner. Choose one of the jobs from the box,
but don't tell your partner. Ask and answer Yes/No questions
to find out what the job is.

receptionist	artist	lawyer	architect	taxi driver	sales assistant	vet
decorator	miner	dancer	detective	soldier	ambulance driver	
mechanic	farmer	dentist	plumber	housewife	fire fighter	

Do you ... ?
- work indoors or outdoors
- earn a lot of money
- work regular hours

Do you have to ... ?
- wear a uniform
- use your hands
- answer the phone

Do you work indoors?

Yes, I do./No, I don't.

3 Which of the jobs *wouldn't* you like to do? Why?

I wouldn't like to be a farmer because they have to work outdoors all year.

Talking about you

4 In groups, discuss the questions. If you live at home with your parents,
use the present tense. If you don't live with your parents anymore, use
the past tense.

1. What $\begin{vmatrix} do \\ did \end{vmatrix}$ you have to do to help around the house? What about
your brothers and sisters?

2. $\begin{vmatrix} Can \\ Could \end{vmatrix}$ you stay out as long as you $\begin{vmatrix} want? \\ wanted? \end{vmatrix}$ Or $\begin{vmatrix} do \\ did \end{vmatrix}$ you have to
be home by a certain time?

3. $\begin{vmatrix} Do \\ Did \end{vmatrix}$ you always have to tell your parents where you $\begin{vmatrix} are \\ were \end{vmatrix}$ going?

4. How strict $\begin{vmatrix} are \\ were \end{vmatrix}$ your parents? What $\begin{vmatrix} do \\ did \end{vmatrix}$ they let you do?

5. What $\begin{vmatrix} do \\ did \end{vmatrix}$ you and your parents argue about?

PROBLEMS, PROBLEMS
should, must

1 Match the problems and suggestions on the right. What advice would *you* give?

2 **T 8.3** Listen and complete the advice. Use the words from the box.

shouldn't	should
must	don't think you should

1. I think you _____ talk to your boss.
2. You _____ drink coffee at night.
3. I _____ go to the wedding.
4. You _____ go to the dentist! Don't wait!

Practice the conversations with a partner. Use the problems on the right and the advice in Exercise 1.

3 Give advice to your friends.
- I'm overweight.
- My cat's sick.
- I have a big test next week.
- I'm always arguing with my parents.
- My parents' wedding anniversary is next week.
- My car's making a funny noise.

GRAMMAR SPOT

1 Which sentence expresses a suggestion? Which sentence expresses strong obligation?
   You should go on a diet.
   You must go to the dentist!

2 *Should* and *must* are modal verbs.
   She **must** get a license before she can drive a car.
   You **shouldn't** smoke. It's bad for you.
   What **should** he do?
   Do we add *-s* with *he/she/it*? Do we use *do/does* in the question and negative?

3 We can make a negative suggestion with *I don't think …*
   I don't think you should drive so fast.

▶▶ **Grammar Reference 8.2–8.4 pp. 147–148**

Problems

I'm working 16 hours a day.

I can't sleep.

My ex-boyfriend's getting married.

I've had a terrible toothache for weeks.

Suggestions

Don't drink coffee at night.

Go to the dentist. Don't wait!

Don't go to the wedding.

Talk to your boss.

PRACTICE

Grammar

1 Make sentences from the chart.

If you want to . . .		
learn English, do well in life, stay healthy,	you have to you don't have to you should you shouldn't	work hard. exercise or play sports. learn the grammar. go to college. buy a dictionary. smoke. believe in yourself. speak your language in class.

A trip to your country

2 Someone is going to stay in your country for six months. What advice can you give?

You should bring warm clothes. **You don't have to get a visa.**
You have to have a passport. **You must try our local speciality.**

Include advice about money, documents, clothes, health, housing, and food.

LISTENING AND SPEAKING
Vacations in January

1 Do many people in your country go on vacation in January? Where do they go? Where would *you* like to go for a January vacation? Write a sentence and read it to the class.

I'd like to go to ... because ...

2 **T 8.4** Listen to Fatima, Ali, and Toni giving advice about visiting their country in the month of January. Who is from Egypt? Who is from Switzerland? Who is from Mexico?

3 **T 8.4** Listen again and complete the chart. Compare your answers with a partner.

	Weather and clothes	Things to do, places to go	Food and drink
Fatima			
Ali			
Toni			

4 Answer the questions.
1. Look at the photographs. Which vacation do they go with?
2. Who talked about money? What did he/she say?
3. Who suggested going on a boat trip? Where?
4. Which of these countries would you like to visit? Why?

Speaking

5 Put the words in the correct order to make questions.
1. weather / is / like / in / what / the / January?
2. take / clothes / what / should / I?
3. can / things / kinds / of / what / do / I?
4. special / any / there / places / are / that / should / visit / I?
5. food / you / recommend / do / what?

6 Choose another vacation destination you know. Ask and answer the questions in Exercise 5.

1 These problems come from a newspaper column where people write in with a problem, and other members of the public give their advice. Read the problems. What advice would you give?

2 Match the readers' letters to these problems. There are two for each problem.

Dilemmas

with **Vanessa Goodman**

THIS WEEK'S PROBLEMS

Do I have to act my age?

Laura is 47. She is single, and her children have left home. She is very successful in her career and has a lot of friends, but she isn't satisfied. She longs to change her life. She wants to live abroad, paint, and write poetry, but her friends tell her she should stop being silly and act her age.

a. ____ ____

Do I have to be a slave to my cell phone?

Jason's company bought him a cell phone. They want him to carry it with him all the time, so that they can contact him anywhere, anytime. He dislikes the idea of always being available, and he hates the way people use cell phones to have private conversations in public.

b. ____ ____

Should I throw my son out?

Sarah's 24-year-old son lives at home, stays in bed until late, and watches TV all day. He's a member of a gang that sometimes causes trouble in the neighborhood. He's intelligent, but he dropped out of school. He's never had a job. His father wants to throw him out, but Sarah worries that he could end up getting into trouble and put in prison.

c. ____ ____

READERS' ADVICE

1 Children always need the support of their parents, whether they're four or twenty-four. I think you should pay for him to get some job training, and when he's ready, _____ find somewhere to live. Meanwhile, _____ him all the love that he needs.

Jenny Wong, *Los Angeles, CA*

2 I decided to give it all up and change my life dramatically three years ago. Since then, _____ the most exciting three years of my life. It can be scary, but if you don't do it, you won't know what you've missed. I don't think _____ . Go for it.

Mike Garfield, *Vancouver, BC, Canada*

3 He's using you. I think _____ . It's time for him to go. Twenty-four is too old to be living with his parents. He has to take responsibility for himself. And _____ about his gang activities. Sometimes you have to be cruel to be kind.

Luis Antonio Cruz, *Miami, FL*

4 Why _____ it? He isn't their slave; they don't own him. And I too can't stand the way people use their cell phones in restaurants and on trains and buses. They think that the people around them are invisible and can't hear. _____ .

Jane Sandowski, *Chicago, IL*

5 I think _____ before she gives up her job and goes to live abroad. Does she think that the sun will always shine? If there is something in her life that makes her unhappy now, this will follow her. She should take her time _____ .

Marie Pucci, *Dallas, TX*

6 _____ ! He should have a talk with his supervisor and come to an agreement. Why can't he turn it off sometimes? Cell phones are great, and if he has one for free, _____ . They are one of the best inventions ever.

Pete Gold, *Phoenix, AR*

3 Where do these lines go? Put the lines into the correct letter.

a. … you should tell him to move out.
b. … she should be very careful …
c. … you should help him …
d. … you should worry.
e. He has to keep it!
f. … before making a decision.
g. It is so rude.
h. … he's very lucky.
i. I have had …
j. … you must tell the police …
k. … you have to give …
l. … should he accept …

T 8.5 Listen and check.

4 Which letter writer … ?

____ suggests waiting

____ thinks love is the answer

____ has been adventurous

____ thinks that employers shouldn't exploit their employees

____ loves cell phones

____ suggests being tough

The readers make very different suggestions. Who do you agree with?

What do you think?

- How old are children when they move out of their parents' home in your country?
- What do you think of people who use cell phones in public?
- Do you think older people should act their age? Why/Why not?
- "You have to be cruel to be kind." Can you think of an example?

Role play

With a partner, choose a situation and role-play the conversation.

- Laura and one of her friends
- Jason and his boss
- Sarah and her husband

Group work

In groups, write a letter to an advice column.

Exchange your letters and write a reply. Try to express sympathy with the problem and give some explanation, as well as practical advice.

VOCABULARY
Words that go together

1 Many verbs and nouns go together.

tell a story   make a decision

Look at the chart on the right. Match a verb with a complement. They all appear in the letters and problems on pages 62–63.

Look at the letters and problems again and check your answers.

2 Close your books. Try to remember the sentences that include the phrases from the box.

3 Two nouns can go together.

| post office   headache   baby-sitter |

The stress is usually on the first word.

Match the nouns to make new words.

Verbs	Complements
live	being silly
write	your age
stop	abroad
act	responsibility for
take	poetry
take	your job
stay	what you've missed
don't know	a talk with someone
have to be	in bed
give up	your time
have	cruel to be kind

alarm	cream	hair	case
movie	glasses	sun	dryer
traffic	break	ear	quake
credit	coat	can	opener
ice	light	book	ring
sun	card	rush	lighter
coffee	star	cigarette	set
rain	clock	earth	hour

T 8.6 Listen and check.

4 Choose a word and give a definition to the class. Can they guess the word?

You use it to pay for things.

That's right.

A credit card.

EVERYDAY ENGLISH
A visit to the doctor

1 Complete the table with an illness or a symptom.

diarrhea food poisoning the flu	It hurts when I walk on it. My glands are swollen, and it hurts when I swallow. I can't stop sneezing, and my nose is runny.

Illnesses	Symptoms
I have a cold.	
I have _____ .	I have a temperature, my whole body aches, and I feel awful.
I twisted my ankle.	
I have _____ .	I keep going to the bathroom.
I have a sore throat.	
I have _____ .	I keep throwing up, and I have diarrhea.

2 Put the sentences in the correct order.

____ She took my temperature and examined me.

____ After a few days, I started to feel better.

_1_ I didn't feel very well.

____ I went to the clinic and saw the doctor.

____ I went to the pharmacy and got the prescription filled.

____ I called the doctor's office and made an appointment.

____ She told me I had an infection.

____ I explained what was wrong.

____ She gave me a prescription for some medication.

3 **T 8.7** You will hear a conversation between Manuel, a student from Chile, and a doctor. Answer the questions.

1. What are Manuel's symptoms?
2. What questions does the doctor ask?
3. What does the doctor think is the matter with Manuel?
4. What does she prescribe?
5. What advice does she give him?
6. Where does he have to go to fill the prescription?

4 Look at the tapescript on page 134. Practice with a partner.

5 Make similar conversations with other symptoms.

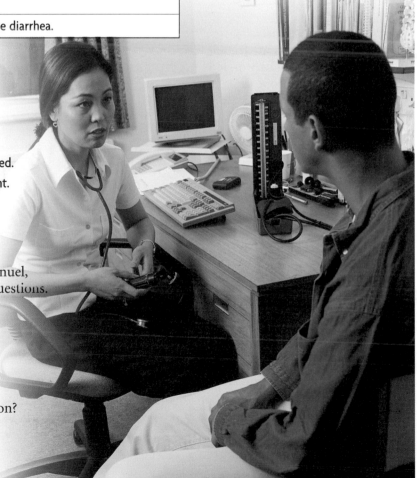

9 Going places

Time clauses · *if* · Hot verbs · In a hotel

STARTER ▶ What will you do if the weather is nice this weekend?
What will you do when you get home tonight?

TAKING A YEAR OFF
Time and conditional clauses

1 Claire and her friend Annie are taking a year off from school to travel. Complete the sentences with phrases from the box below.

1. We're traveling around the world **before we go to college.**
2. We're going to leave …
3. When we're in Australia, …
4. If we get sick, …
5. After we leave Australia, …
6. We can stay with my friends …
7. Our parents will be worried …
8. We'll stay in Europe …

---

a. while we're in Madrid.
b. we'll take care of each other.
c. before we go to college.
d. until we run out of money.
e. we're going to learn to scuba dive on the Great Barrier Reef.
f. as soon as we have enough money.
g. we're going to Europe.
h. if we don't stay in touch.

T 9.1 Listen and check.

2 Cover the box. Practice the sentences.

GRAMMAR SPOT

1 Underline the words above that introduce the clauses, for example, *while*.

2 What tenses are the verbs in the box? Do they refer to the present or the future?

3 What are the different future forms in Claire and Annie's sentences?

4 What's the difference between these sentences? Which one is sure? Which one is possible?
   When I get home, I'll have something to eat.
   If there isn't any food, I'll get a pizza.

▶▶ **Grammar Reference 9.1–9.3 p. 148**

PRACTICE

when, as soon as

1 Complete the sentences with your ideas.

1 When I get home ...

2 As soon as this class is over ...

3 If I win ...

4 After I finish high school ...

5 While I'm in New York ...

6 ... before I get too old.

T 9.2 Listen and compare your answers.

What if ... ?

2 Look at these hopes for the future. Make sentences using *If ..., will ...*

If I don't go out so much, I'll do more work.
If I do more work, I'll ...

IF ...

I don't go out so much
↓
do more work
↓
pass my exams
↓
go to medical school
↓
study medicine
↓
become a doctor
↓
make a good salary.

IF ...

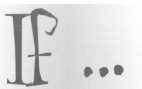

I stop smoking
↓
have more money
↓
save some every week
↓
be rich when I'm 30
↓
have my own business
↓
make a lot of money
↓
retire when I'm 40.

What will you do?

3 Work with a partner. One of you is going skiing for the first time. The other sees all the problems. Use these ideas to help you.

What will you do if there's no snow?

We'll go for a walk.

- don't like the food
- it rains
- don't learn to ski
- hurt yourself

- there's nothing to do in the evening
- don't make any friends
- lose your money
- get lost in a snowstorm

Make a similar conversation about going on safari for the first time.

Discussing grammar

4 Complete the sentences with *when, if, before,* or *until*.

1. I'll take a bath **before** I go to bed.
2. I'm going to Taipei tomorrow. I'll call you _____ I arrive.
3. _____ it's a nice day tomorrow, we can go swimming.
4. Wait here _____ I get back.
5. _____ you have any problems, just ask for help.
6. I want to get home _____ it gets dark.
7. I'm going to take driving lessons _____ I pass my test.
8. Give me your address _____ you go home.

When I get to Vancouver …

5 Put the verbs in parentheses in the correct tense. Put *if, when, while,* or *as soon as* into each box.

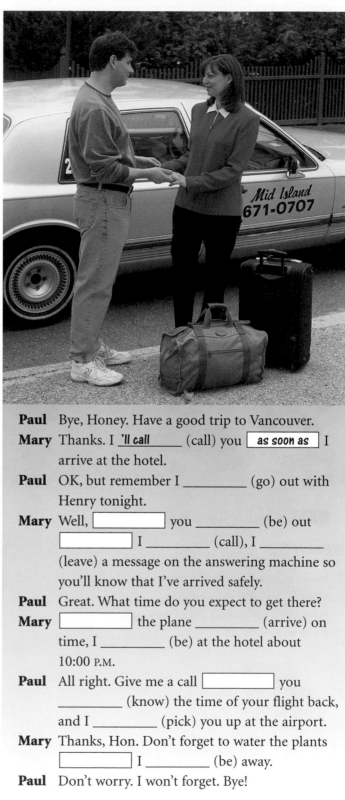

Paul Bye, Honey. Have a good trip to Vancouver.

Mary Thanks. I **'ll call** (call) you **as soon as** I arrive at the hotel.

Paul OK, but remember I _____ (go) out with Henry tonight.

Mary Well, [_____] you _____ (be) out [_____] I _____ (call), I _____ (leave) a message on the answering machine so you'll know that I've arrived safely.

Paul Great. What time do you expect to get there?

Mary [_____] the plane _____ (arrive) on time, I _____ (be) at the hotel about 10:00 P.M.

Paul All right. Give me a call [_____] you _____ (know) the time of your flight back, and I _____ (pick) you up at the airport.

Mary Thanks, Hon. Don't forget to water the plants [_____] I _____ (be) away.

Paul Don't worry. I won't forget. Bye!

T 9.3 Listen and check.

LISTENING AND SPEAKING
Life in the 21st century

1 Think of some of the inventions and discoveries of the 19th and 20th centuries, such as electricity and computers. How have they changed people's lives?

2 How do you think science will change our lives during the 21st century? Check that you know these words.

> the Internet   DNA   genes   robots   solar energy

3 **T 9.4** Listen to two students discussing a book called *Visions: How Science Will Revolutionize the 21st Century*. Take notes on their discussion.

4 Answer the questions about the predictions in *Visions*.

1. What will computers be like in the future? What about the Internet?
2. What will robots be able to do?
3. Will scientists understand DNA? What effect will that have on medicine?
4. What other medical advances will there be?
5. How long will some people live?
6. What kind of energy will people use? What about cars?
7. What about space travel?

What do you think?

Do you agree with all the predictions? What other scientific discoveries and inventions do you think will happen in the 21st century and beyond? Will all these advances be good for us? Why or why not?

READING AND SPEAKING
The world's first megalopolis

1 Look at the pictures and read the introduction to the article on this page. How can a city be "an ugly, exciting mess"?

2 Read the magazine article about Pearl River City on page 71. Why is it ugly? Why is it exciting?

3 On the map, find the following:
- Pearl River Estuary ___2___
- Shenzhen ___
- Guangzhou ___
- the Hopewell Highway ___

4 Answer the questions.
1. Does the city have a name yet?
2. What are some of the statistics about Shenzhen that make it a remarkable place?
3. In what ways is China changing? Why were Deng Xiaoping's words significant?
4. How are the people changing? Why do they want to own cars?
5. What does Shenzhen look like?
6. Why will this city be important in the twenty-first century?
7. What do these numbers refer to?

1982	thousands
3 million	six months
less than ten years	two hours
40 million	four hours

What do you think?

- In groups, write what you think are the ten largest cities in the world. Compare your list with the class. Then check your answers on page 123.

- Make a list of some of the problems that these cities face. Decide which are the three most important problems. Compare your ideas with the class.

Overcrowding is a big problem.

To the north of Hong Kong, the world's biggest city is growing. It has no name yet, but it will probably be called Pearl River City. Jonathon Glancey visits this ugly, exciting mess.

Megalopolis

The town of Shenzhen, just 40 kilometers north of Hong Kong, is the world's biggest building site. In 1982 it was a fishing village with two main roads, fields, and a population of 30,000. Now it has a population of 3 million. It is growing at an incredible speed. It is spreading north toward Guangzhou (formerly known as Canton) and west toward Macau. The Chinese government hopes that in less than 10 years this area will be the biggest city on earth, with a population of 40 million people.

China is changing. It is no longer a country where absolutely everything is owned and controlled by the state. Developers are welcome. As Deng Xiaoping, the Chinese leader, said in 1992, "To get rich is glorious." The old China of bicycles and Little Red Books is disappearing. A world of wireless phones and capitalism is arriving.

The Chinese people seem to welcome dramatic change. They don't worry about losing traditional ways of life. They want the new. As the posters on the sides of the highways shout, "Development is the only way."

Shenzhen is a shocking place, like nowhere else on earth that I have ever seen. It is a city with no boundaries and no center. There are new concrete office buildings, factories, and apartment buildings as far as the eye can see. Not just dozens of new buildings, nor even hundreds, but thousands. And it is all happening so fast. It takes just 6 months to design, build, and finish a 60-story, air-conditioned skyscraper. As one architect said to me, "If you move too slowly here, someone will walk over you."

The new Hopewell Highway runs from Shenzhen to Guangzhou, and it takes just 2 hours to do the 123 kilometers. This superhighway will become the main street of a huge new city, as it gets bigger and bigger until the east meets the west, and the countryside in the middle disappears under concrete.

There will of course be more and more cars on the road. People don't want bicycles. If you have a car, it means you have made money. So the traffic will be like in Bangkok, where people spend four hours commuting every day. People eat and do their work in their cars.

Pearl River City very nearly exists. It will probably be the world's First City, the greatest city on earth. It won't be beautiful, but its power, energy, and wealth will be felt in all corners of the world.

VOCABULARY
Hot verbs—*take, get, do, make*

1 The verbs *take, get, do,* and *make* are very common in English. Find these examples in the text about China:

> **get** rich   it **gets** bigger and bigger   you have **made** money
> it **takes** two hours   **do** their work

2 Here are some more examples of *take, get, do,* and *make*.

A How long does it take you to get ready in the morning?
B It takes me about 15 minutes.

A How long does it take you to get to school?
B I can get here in 20 minutes.

A Do you get tired in the evening?
B Yes. Especially after I've done a lot of homework.

A Do you make a lot of mistakes in English?
B Well, I do my best, but I still make a few mistakes.

Ask and answer the same questions with a partner.

3 Put the words and phrases from the box in the correct column.

some shopping	friends	back home	along well with someone
up your mind	angry	sure	a reservation
me a favor	care	a photo	somebody out for dinner
a complaint	a pill	a cold	

TAKE	GET	DO	MAKE
a pill			

4 Complete the sentences with one of the verb phrases from Exercise 3. Use the correct form of the verb.

1. I _____ while I was in town. I bought myself a new sweater.
2. "I don't know if I love Tom or Henry." "_____ . You can't marry both of them."
3. Bye-bye! See you soon. _____ of yourself.
4. Aachoo! Oh, no! I think I'm _____ .
5. "Are the doors locked?" "I think so, but I'll just _____ ."

T 9.5 Listen and check.

5 Discuss these questions with a partner.

- How long does it take to get from your school to the nearest train station or bus stop? From your home to work?
- When did you last do someone a favor/make a complaint/take a photo/get angry?
- What time did you get home last night?
- Do you get along with your parents/your neighbors?
- Is it easy for you to make friends?

72   Unit 9 · Going places

EVERYDAY ENGLISH
In a hotel

1 What is the best hotel in your city or town? What facilities does the hotel have?

2 Ask and answer questions with a partner about the Molokai Grand Hotel.

> Where's the conference center?

> On the third floor.

The Molokai Grand Hotel
★★★★

Lobby	Front Desk/Reception
	City Bar
Second Floor	Coffee Shop
	Waterfall Rooms
Third Floor	Conference Center
Top Floor	Panorama Restaurant
Basement	Fitness Center
	Swimming pool/spa

3 Put the words in the right order from the telephone conversation between the receptionist and guest.

Receptionist Thank you for calling the Molokai Grand Hotel. Cathy speaking. How can I help you?

Guest reservation / make / like / a / I'd / to

_____ .

Receptionist For what dates?

Guest It's for two nights, the thirteenth and fourteenth of this month.

Receptionist single / want / do / room / or / double / a / And / you / a

_____ ?

Guest A single. Non-smoking if it's available.

Receptionist OK. Yes, that's fine. I have a room for you. And your name is?

Guest Robert Palmer.

what / you / Can / tell / the / is / me / rate

_____ ?

Receptionist Yes. That's $150 a night. Would you like to guarantee your reservation with a credit card?

Guest Yes, sure. It's a Visa. 4929 7983 0621 8849.

Receptionist Thank you.

number / could / And / telephone / please / I / have / a

_____ ?

Guest Uh-huh. It's 954-915-0970.

Receptionist You're all set, Mr. Palmer.

forward / look / seeing / on / you / We / to / thirtcenth / the

_____ . Bye-bye.

Guest Thanks a lot. Good-bye.

[T 9.6] Listen and check.

4 With a partner, role-play the conversation between Robert Palmer and the receptionist as he checks in to the hotel.

> *Good evening. How can I help you?*

> *Hello. I have a reservation. My name's Robert Palmer.*

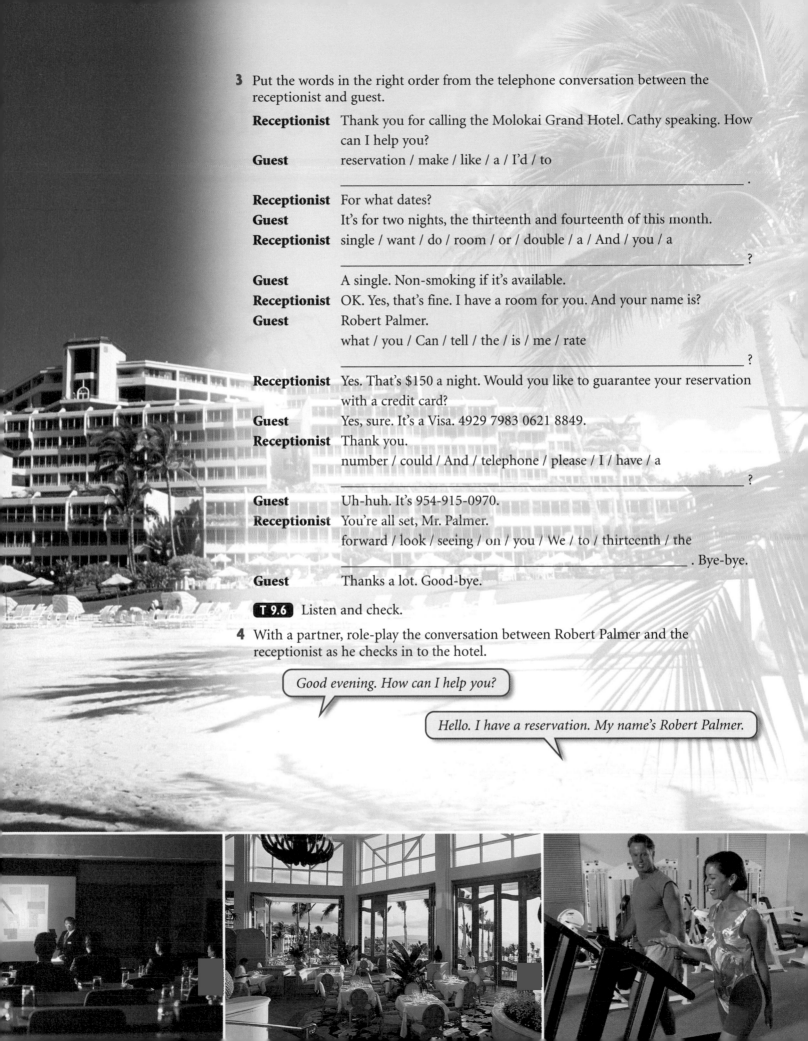

10 Scared to death

STARTER

1 What are these people afraid of? How do they feel?

2 What are you afraid of? Why?

A WALK WITH DEATH
Verb patterns and infinitives

1 Look at the photograph on page 75. Does the path look safe to you?

Read about Paul Lay's adventure. How did he feel at different times in the story?

2 Complete the text using these words.

> began to feel   started aching
> know what to do   went camping
> decided to stand up

T 10.1 Listen and check.

3 Answer the questions.
 1. What is Paul Lay's hobby?
 2. What did he use to do with his father?
 3. Does he go to the same place every year?
 4. Is the King's Way in good condition?
 5. Why couldn't he take a rest?
 6. Why didn't he enjoy the walk?

Don't look down

Paul Lay dances with death in the mountains of southern Spain

I have always enjoyed walking. When I was a boy, I used to go walking on weekends with my father. We (1) _____ and climbing together.

I try to visit a new place every year. Last year I decided to walk a path in Spain called *El camino del rey*, which means the King's Way. It is one of the highest and most dangerous footpaths in Europe. It used to be very safe, but now it's falling down.

I took a train to the village of El Chorro and started to walk toward the mountains. I was very excited. Then the adventure began.

The path was about three feet [one meter] wide, and there were holes in it. It used to have a handrail, but not any more. I didn't (2) _____— should I go on my hands and knees, or stand up? I (3) _____ and walk very slowly. At times the path was only as wide as my two boots. I stopped to take a rest, but there was nowhere to sit.

I (4) _____ very frightened. It was impossible to look down or look up. I was concentrating so hard that my body (5) _____ . There was no thrill of danger, no enjoyment of the view. I thought I was going to die.

I finally managed to get to the end. I was shaking, and I was covered in sweat from heat and fear. I fell to the ground, exhausted.

PRACTICE

Discussing grammar

1 Complete these sentences with the verb *ski* in the correct form.

   1. I go ___*skiing*___ every winter.
   2. I started _____ when I was six.
   3. I tried _____ down the mountain, but it was too steep.
   4. My instructor made me _____ down the steep mountain.
   5. I enjoy _____ very much.
   6. Dave used to _____ when he was younger, but not anymore.

2 Choose the correct form.

   1. I decided *stop* / *(to stop)* / *stopping* smoking.
   2. I managed *find* / *to find* / *finding* my passport.
   3. Let's go *shop* / *to shop* / *shopping*!
   4. I tried *understand* / *to understand* / *understanding* what he was saying, but I couldn't.
   5. Would you like something *eat* / *to eat* / *eating*?
   6. I need a recipe for a cake that's easy *make* / *to make* / *making*.

When I was young, I used to ...

3 **T 10.2** Listen to Jim talking about his childhood and his life now. Complete the chart. Write one sentence with *used to* for each question.

	Life as a child
1. What/do on weekends?	
2. What/do in the evening?	
3. Where/go on vacation?	
4. What sports/play?	
5. What TV programs/like?	
6. What food/like?	

Jim

With a partner, ask and answer the questions above about your life now and your life as a child.

> *What do you do on weekends?*

> *I usually go shopping and ...*

> *What did you do when you were a child?*

> *I used to play with my friends and ...*

Infinitives

4 Why do you go to these places?

> *Why do you go to the hairstylist?*

> *To get a haircut.*

- the post office
- a gas station
- a bookstore
- the newsstand
- the library
- the supermarket

With your partner, ask and answer questions about more places.

5 Make sentences with a line in **A**, a word in **B**, and an infinitive in **C**.

A	B	C
1. I'm hungry. I need	how	to say to you.
2. My CD player's broken. Can you show me	anything	to talk to.
3. Don't talk to me. I have	which way	to eat.
4. Do I turn left or right? I don't know	somebody	to wear.
5. I'm bored. I don't have	how much	to fix it?
6. "Can you get some milk?" "Sure. Tell me	nothing	to do.
7. I feel lonely. I need	something	to go.
8. I'm going to a formal party, but I don't know	what	to buy."

T 10.3 Think of some replies. Then listen and compare your answers.

Check it

6 Choose the correct form.

1. I went shopping *for to buy / for buy / to buy* some shoes.
2. Do you enjoy *dance / dancing / to dance*?
3. When I was young, I used *to go / go / going* ice-skating.
4. He told me he loves me. I didn't know what *say / to say / saying*.
5. When we were on vacation, we went *swim / to swim / swimming* every day.

VOCABULARY
-ed/-ing adjectives

1 How can you describe these experiences? Use an adjective from the box.

frightening exciting surprising terrifying boring exhausting

1. You get stuck in an elevator. *frightening, terrifying*
2. You go on a 25-km hike, then climb three mountains.
3. You go on the biggest roller coaster in the world.
4. You find a spider in the bathtub.
5. Someone shows you their vacation photos for hours and hours.
6. Your teacher says, "You're all such wonderful students that I won't give you any more homework."

2 How do think the people in the photos feel?

He looks frightened.

T 10.4 Listen and practice the pronunciation of these words.

> ❗ 1 **-ing** adjectives describe a situation, person, or thing.
>   an **interesting** teacher
>   a **boring** movie
>   an **exciting** life
>
> 2 **-ed** adjectives describe how people feel.
>   I'm very **interested** in modern art.
>   We were **bored** at the end of the lesson.
>   She's **excited** about going on vacation tomorrow.

3 Complete the sentences. Use one of these adjectives.

| excit-
frighten-
bor-
interest-
confus-
disappoint-
worry/worri-
surpris- | -ed

-ing |
|---|---|

1. "I met a famous actor today." "Really? How _____ !"
2. "I spent four hours walking around a museum today." "Was it _____ ?"
   "No, it was _____ ."
3. "I haven't heard from my parents for two months." "You must be _____ ."
4. "Ann! I can't believe you're here!" "Why are you so _____ to see me?"
5. I failed the exam. I studied really hard for it. I'm so _____ .
6. "A man started to follow me home last night." "Weren't you _____ ?"
7. My computer's broken, and I don't understand the manual. It's so _____ .

T 10.5 Close your books. Listen to the beginnings of the lines. Complete them.

4 What have you seen on television or in the movies recently? What books have you read? What did you think of them? Tell a partner.

> *I read a spy novel. It was very exciting.*

> *I saw a horror movie. I thought it was frightening.*

READING AND SPEAKING
Into the wild

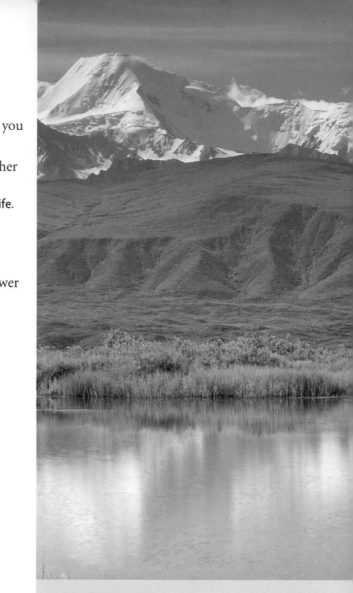

1 Describe what you can see in the photographs. Which country do you think it is? What makes life difficult for people who live here?

2 Look at the text and read the words in **bold**. In pairs, decide whether these statements are true (✔) or false (✗).

- ☐ Chris McCandless died very young.
- ☐ He was killed by hunters.
- ☐ He didn't enjoy his life.
- ☐ He loved nature and a simple life.
- ☐ He wanted to die.
- ☐ He knew he was dying.

What do you want to know about Chris?

3 Read to the line ending "' … *Thank you!' his diary reads.*" and answer the questions.

1. Did Chris stay in touch with his parents? When did they last hear from him?
2. Why did he get rid of his car and burn his money?
3. What did he need? What didn't he need?
4. In what way was his life rich?

4 Read to the line ending " … *I didn't know where he was.*" Choose the best answer.

1. Chris didn't get along with his father because his father
   - ☐ had a lot of money.
   - ☐ didn't let Chris work in the family business.
   - ☐ tried to tell Chris what to do.

2. When the parents didn't hear from Chris,
   - ☐ the police got in touch with them.
   - ☐ they got in touch with the police.
   - ☐ they did nothing.

3. In July 1992
   - ☐ his mother dreamed that she heard Chris calling her.
   - ☐ his mother is sure that she heard Chris calling her.
   - ☐ Chris phoned his mother for help.

5 Read to the end of the article. Correct this summary. There are ten mistakes.

> Chris ~~took the train~~ *hitchhiked* to Alaska and arrived in May, 1992. He lived in a bus, and there was a bed and a bath in it. He was very happy. There was lots to eat—small animals, and fruits and vegetables, which he grew himself.
>
> After five months of living alone, he started to feel ill. He had no strength because he was eating poisonous plants, and he knew this was the reason. He continued eating. He died of food poisoning.
>
> He knew he was dying. He wrote a letter to his parents and took a photo of himself. He seemed happy to die under these circumstances.

What do you think?

- What was important to Chris? What wasn't important?
- What do you think he was trying to do?
- Why do young people feel the need to break away from their parents?

In April 1992, Chris McCandless, a young man from a wealthy family, hitchhiked to Alaska. Four months later, his dead body was found by a group of hunters. Jon Krakauer investigated the story.

When Chris McCandless graduated from Emory University in Atlanta, Georgia, in June 1990, he sent his parents a letter containing his final grades. His letter ended "Say 'Hi' to everyone for me."

No one in Chris's family ever heard from him again.

He drove west out of Atlanta and invented a new life for himself with a new name. He left his car in some woods and burned all his money, because, as he wrote in his diary, "**I need no possessions. I can survive with just nature.**"

For the next two years, he hitchhiked to various parts of the United States and

Into the wild

Mexico. He wanted the freedom to go where he wanted and to work when he needed. For him, his life was very rich. **"God, it's great to be alive. Thank you! Thank you!"** his diary reads.

Chris came from a comfortable background. His father had a business which he ran efficiently, and he controlled his own family in a similar way. Chris and his father didn't get along. When his parents didn't hear from him for several months, they contacted the police, but they could do nothing. In July 1992, two years after Chris left Atlanta, his mother woke up in the middle of the night. "I could hear Chris calling me. I wasn't dreaming. He was begging, 'Mom! Help me!' But I couldn't help him because I didn't know where he was."

Chris's dream was to spend some time in Alaska, and this is where he went in April 1992. In early May, after a few days in the Alaskan wilderness, Chris found an old bus which hunters used for shelter. It had a bed and a stove. He decided to stay there for a while. **"Total freedom,"** he wrote. **"My home is the road."**

> I need no possessions. I can survive with just nature.

However, reality soon changed the dream. He was hungry, and it was difficult to find enough to eat. He shot ducks, squirrels, birds, and sometimes a moose, and with these he ate wild potatoes, wild mushrooms, and berries. He was losing a lot of weight.

On July 30 he wrote, **"Extremely weak. Fault of potato seed. Can't stand up. Starving. Danger."** It seems that Chris was eating a part of the wild potato plant that was poisonous. He couldn't get out of the bus to look for food. **"I am trapped in the wild,"** he wrote on August 5.

He became weaker and weaker as he was starving to death. His final note says, **"I have had a good life and thank the Lord. Good-bye and may God bless all!"**

Then he crawled into his sleeping bag and lost consciousness. He probably died on August 18. One of the last things he did was to take a photo of himself, one hand holding his final note, the other hand raised in a brave good-bye. His face is horribly thin, but he is smiling in the picture, and the look in his eyes says "I am at peace."

LISTENING AND SPEAKING

It came from the sky!

1 Some people say they have seen UFOs (Unidentified Flying Objects).

- What do they say UFOs look like?
- What stories do you know about flying saucers?

2 Work with a partner. You are going to listen to a man who says that he has seen a UFO, spoken with the aliens in it, and been inside their spacecraft. Write five questions you would like to ask him.

Where were you?
What did the aliens look like?

3 **T 10.6** You will hear a man named Peter Cooper describe his encounter with a UFO. Listen to the interview and put the pictures in the right order. Check that you know these words.

| metallic   government agent   helmet   visor   to land   to take off |

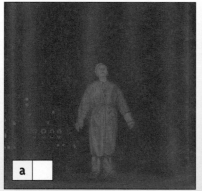

a

b

c

d

e

f

g

4 **T 10.6** Listen again. Did Mr. Cooper answer any of your questions from Exercise 2?

5 What do the following refer to in the story?

1. about a year ago
   He saw the UFO about a year ago.
2. one o'clock
3. full
4. green
5. a machine
6. 45 feet
7. shiny
8. black
9. a minute
10. seventy-four

What do you think?

- Do you think people will believe Mr. Cooper's story? Why or why not?
- The government agent told Mr. Cooper, "Don't tell anyone about this." If UFOs were real, do you think the government would tell us? Why or why not?

Role play

Work with a partner. Role-play <u>one</u> of these conversations.

- Mr. Cooper talking to a neighbor
- Mr. Cooper talking to someone from the government
- Mr. Cooper talking to a reporter

EVERYDAY ENGLISH
Exclamations with *so* and *such*

1 **T 10.7** Read and listen to the sentences.
Mr. Cooper was scared.   *He was very scared.*   *He was so scared!*

2 Look at the sentences. When do we use *so*, *such a(n)*, *such*, *so many*, and *so much*?

> We were all *so worried*!
> That's *such an old joke*!
> It was *such a beautiful night*!
> He has *such crazy friends*!
> We had *such awful weather* on vacation!
> There are *so many places* I want to go to!
> I have *so much work*!

3 Complete the sentences in **A** with *so*, *such a*, *such*, *so many*, or *so much*. Then match them with the sentences in **B**.

A	B
1. Their house is ___such a___ mess!	I could eat a horse.
2. There were _____ people at the party!	I don't know where it all went.
3. I'm _____ hungry!	You really didn't have to.
4. Jane and Pete are _____ nice people!	She understands every word I say.
5. I spent _____ money this weekend!	There was nowhere to dance.
6. A present! For me? That's _____ sweet!	Thank you so much for inviting us.
7. We had _____ good time!	But I can't stand their kids.
8. Princess is _____ smart dog!	I don't know how they can live in it.

T 10.8 Listen and check. Practice the exclamations.

4 What can you say … ?

- at the end of a long trip

That was such a long trip!

I'm so tired!

- when you finish an interesting book with a sad ending
- when you visit a friend's new apartment
- at the end of a wonderful meal
- in an argument with your boyfriend/girlfriend
- at the end of a great English class

11 Things that changed the world

Passives • Verbs and nouns that go together • Signs and notices

1 Make true sentences from the chart.
2 What is made and grown in your region or country?

Rolls-Royce cars Nikon cameras Coffee Champagne Tea Pineapples	is are	made in grown in	Japan. France. Thailand. Brazil. India. England.

SOLD WORLDWIDE
Passives

1 Do you drink Coca-Cola? Do you think these facts about Coca-Cola are true (✓) or false (✗)?

1. ☐ 1.6 billion gallons (about 6 billion liters) are sold every day.
2. ☐ Coca-Cola is drunk in every country in the world.
3. ☐ It was invented in the United States.
4. ☐ It is nearly 100 years old.

Read the story of Coca-Cola and check your ideas.

Things go better with Coca-Cola

Coca-Cola is enjoyed all over the world.

1.6 billion gallons are sold every year, in over 160 countries. The drink was invented by Dr. John Pemberton in Atlanta, Georgia, as a health drink on May 8, 1886, but it was given the name Coca-Cola by his partner, Frank Robinson. In the first year, only nine drinks a day were sold.

The business was bought by a man named Asa Candler in 1888, and the first factory was opened in Dallas, Texas, in 1895. Coca-Cola is still made there. Billions of bottles and cans have been produced since 1895, but the recipe has been kept a secret!

Diet Coke has been made since 1982, and over the years many creative advertisements have been used to sell the product. It is certain that Coca-Cola will be drunk far into the twenty-first century.

"Coca-Cola" and "Coke" are registered trademarks which identify the same product of The Coca-Cola Company.

Coca-Cola goes along…for *the pause that refreshes*

GRAMMAR SPOT

1 Nearly all the verb forms in the text about Coca-Cola are in the passive. The passive is formed with the verb *to be* and the past participle.

Champagne **is made** in France.
Pineapples **are grown** in Thailand.

2 Read the text again and write all the passive verb forms in the correct column below.

Present Simple	Past Simple	Present Perfect	*will* Future
is enjoyed	was invented	have been produced	

3 What is the main focus of the text? Dr. John Pemberton? Frank Robinson? Coca-Cola?

When we are more interested in the object of an active sentence, we use the passive.

Active: Dr. John Pemberton invented Coca-Cola.
Passive: Coca-Cola was invented by Dr. John Pemberton.

▶▶ **Grammar Reference 11.1 p. 150**

2 Don't look at the text! Look at the passive verb forms in the columns above and try to remember the whole sentence.

Coca-Cola is enjoyed all over …

It was invented by …

PRACTICE

Active and passive

1 Complete these sentences.

Active	Passive
1. They make Rolls-Royce cars in England.	Rolls-Royce cars _are made_ in England.
2. They _____ tea in India.	Tea is grown in India.
3. Bell invented the telephone in 1876.	The telephone _____ by Bell in 1876.
4. Thieves _____ two pictures from the museum last night.	Two pictures were stolen from the museum last night.
5. They have built three new factories this year.	Three new factories _____ this year.
6. They _____ the picture for $5,000.	The picture has been sold for $5,000.
7. The factory will produce 10,000 cars next year.	10,000 cars _____ next year.
8. _____ they _____ many cars last year?	Were many cars made last year?
9. Bell didn't invent the television.	The television _____ by Bell.

2 Put the verbs in parentheses in the correct tense, active or passive, in the text below.

The History of the Hamburger

The hamburger is eaten more than any other food in the whole world. The first hamburgers (1)**were made** (make) and sold in Connecticut in 1895 by an American chef named Louis Lassen. Louis (2) _____ (call) them hamburgers because he (3) _____ (give) the recipe by sailors from Hamburg, Germany. Hamburgers (4) _____ (become) a favorite in the United States in the early part of the twentieth century. Their popularity (5) _____ (grow) even more after the Second World War, when they (6) _____ (buy) in large quantities by teenagers who (7) _____ (prefer) fast food to family meals. In 1948 two brothers, Dick and Mac McDonald, (8) _____ (open) a drive-in hamburger restaurant in California. Since then over 26,000 McDonald's restaurants (9) _____ (open) worldwide and now 35 million McDonald's hamburgers (10) _____ (eat) every day in 120 countries around the world.

Questions and answers

3 Match the question words and answers.

When?	Louis Lassen.
Where?	In Connecticut.
Who?	In 1895.
Why?	In 1948.
How many?	Because the recipe came from Hamburg.
	Over 26,000.
	35 million.

4 Complete the questions using the passive. Ask and answer them with a partner.

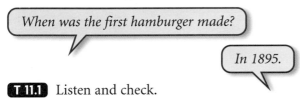

When was the first hamburger made?

In 1895.

T 11.1 Listen and check.

5 Complete the conversations and practice them with a partner.

Is tea grown in France?

No, it isn't. It's grown in India and China.

1. **A** Are Coca-Cola and hamburgers sold *only* in the United States?
   B No, they <u>aren't.</u> <u>They're sold</u> all over the world.
2. **A** Was Coca-Cola invented by Louis Lassen?
   B No, it _____ . _____ by John Pemberton.
3. **A** Were the first hamburgers made in 1948?
   B No, they _____ . _____ in 1895.
4. **A** Was the first McDonald's restaurant opened in New York City?
   B No, it _____ . _____ in San Bernardino, California.
5. **A** Have 2,600 restaurants now been opened worldwide?
   B No, not 2,600. Over 26,000 _____ worldwide.

T 11.2 Listen and check.

Check it

6 <u>Underline</u> the correct word or words in each sentence.

1. Where *was / were* these shoes made?
2. I was given this watch *by / from* my aunt.
3. Someone *has stolen / has been stolen* my bag!
4. The post office *sells / is sold* stamps.
5. British police *don't carry / aren't carried* guns.
6. Have all the sandwiches *eaten / been eaten*?

VOCABULARY
Verbs and nouns that go together

1 In each box below, one noun does *not* go with the verb. Which one?

2 Work with a partner. Choose two nouns from each box above, and write two sentences using the verb. Read your sentences to the class.

Rice is grown in Japan.

My husband is growing a beard.

3 Which nouns don't go with the verbs in Exercise 1 above? Which verbs do they go with? Complete the sentences with the correct verbs.

send say make miss have wear

1. _____ hello to your parents for me when you see them.
2. I was late for work because I _____ the bus.
3. This was my great-grandfather's watch. He _____ it every day for 45 years.
4. I _____ a good idea. Let's eat out tonight.
5. My uncle _____ $3,000 in the stock market.
6. I _____ an e-mail to my cousin in Chicago last week.

READING AND SPEAKING
Three plants that changed the world

1 Read the text below. What is the book about?

Seeds of Change
By Henry Hobhouse

History books are full of the ways in which the actions of men and women have changed the world, but what about plants? Which plants have changed history? Henry Hobhouse, farmer and journalist, discusses this topic in his fascinating and illuminating book *Seeds of Change*.

2 All the words below appear in the texts about the plants. Which words do you think go with which plant? Some go with more than one.

Nouns	addict soil fabric silk plantation slaves lung cancer luxury
Verbs	chain-smoking inhale ban sweeten refine chew harvest

Cotton   **Tobacco**   **Sugar cane**

3 Work in three groups.
Group A Read about tobacco. **Group B** Read about sugar. **Group C** Read about cotton.

4 Which words from Exercise 2 are in your text? What are the bad effects of the plant? What are the good effects? Discuss in your group.

5 Compare plants with two students from the other groups. Answer the questions.

Which plant (or plants) ...
- has been grown for thousands of years?
- was known as "white gold"? Why?
- was once thought to be a luxury?
- was one of the causes of the American Civil War? Why?
- was the main American export until 1820?
- became the main American export after 1820?
- was harvested by slaves?
- has caused the death of many people?

What do you think?

- Which of the three plants has *most* changed history? How?
- Which plant has done the greatest good? Which has done the greatest harm?

Tobacco

For thousands of years **tobacco** was used by the American Indians. In the sixteenth century it was brought to Europe. This early tobacco was mixed with soil and was rather dirty. It was chewed or smoked in pipes only by men—women thought it was smelly and disgusting.

Tobacco was first grown commercially in the United States in the 17th century on large plantations and harvested by slaves. In the 18th century new technology refined tobacco and the first cigarettes were produced. By the 1880s huge factories were producing cigarettes which were easy to smoke. Chain-smoking and inhaling became possible and by the middle of the 20th century tobacco addicts, both men and women, were dying of lung cancer in great numbers.

Nowadays cigarette smoking is banned in many public places, especially in the United States. But until 1820 tobacco was the main export of the United States, and still today the tobacco industry makes over $4.2 billion a year.

Sugar

Sugar cane was grown in India thousands of years ago. In Roman times it was known in Europe as a great luxury, and it was rare and expensive for many centuries after that. In 1493 Columbus took a sugar plant with him to the West Indies, where it grew so well that huge plantations were started by Europeans and worked on by slaves. The slaves were shipped across the Atlantic from Africa, packed sometimes one on top of the other in chains, on a journey that took six weeks. Many died. The empty ships then carried the sugar back to Europe. So much money was made that sugar was known as "white gold."

Sugar is used to sweeten food and make candy, soft drinks, and chocolate. It is addictive but unnecessary. By the 16th century, the English were the greatest sugar-eaters in history. Queen Elizabeth I lost *all* her teeth because she ate so much of it.

Cotton

Cotton has been grown for thousands of years in places as far apart as Mexico, China, Egypt, and India. American colonists started to grow cotton in the early 1600s. Before 1800 cotton was a great luxury, more expensive than silk, because so many workers were needed to pick it. However, a huge increase in the number of slaves in the American South resulted in much greater cotton production and a fall in the price. This, and the new technology of the industrial revolution, made cotton the cheapest fabric in history. By 1820 cotton was making more money for the United States than tobacco, and more money worldwide than sugar.

Many Southern farmers and plantation owners believed that slave labor was necessary for them to make money growing cotton. However many Northerners were opposed to slavery, and this conflict became one cause of the American Civil War (1861–1865), one of the bloodiest wars in American history.

LISTENING AND SPEAKING

The world's most common habit: chewing gum

1 Do you chew gum? How often? Stand up and ask the students in the class. Complete the chart below.

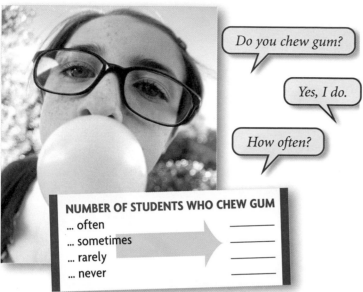

Do you chew gum?

Yes, I do.

How often?

NUMBER OF STUDENTS WHO CHEW GUM

... often	_____
... sometimes	_____
... rarely	_____
... never	_____

2 Discuss these questions as a class.

1. Who often chews gum? Who never chews gum?
2. When and where do you chew gum?
3. Where do you put it after it loses its flavor?

3 You are going to listen to a radio program about chewing gum. Check the meaning of these words. Which ones have an obvious connection with the topic of chewing gum? How?

skeleton *(n)*	to freshen (the breath) *(v)*	tree sap *(n)*
honey *(n)*	to wrap *(v)*	pack *(n)*
to hire *(v)*	billboard *(n)*	chum *(n)*

4 Read the statements below. Do you think they are true (✓) or false (✗)? Discuss with a partner.

1. One million tons of gum are chewed every year.
2. Chewing gum was invented in Sweden.
3. Chewing gum was found in the mouth of a 9,000-year-old skeleton.
4. The first gum was made of tree sap and sugar.
5. Babies are born wanting to chew gum.
6. The ancient Greeks believed chewing gum was good for your health.
7. South American Indians made the first packs of chewing gum.
8. Chewing gum was taken to North America by the English settlers.

T 11.3 Listen to Part One of the program and check your ideas in Exercise 4 above. Correct the false sentences.

5 **T 11.4** Listen to Part Two of the program. Answer the questions.

1. Who was William Wrigley?
2. What did he do to advertise chewing gum?
3. When did chewing gum become popular outside the United States?
4. What did the children shout?
5. What is today's chewing gum made of?

What do you think?

- Is chewing gum a common habit in your country?
- Is it considered a bad habit? Why/Why not?
- Is chewing gum good for you? Why/Why not?

EVERYDAY ENGLISH

Signs and notices

1 When you first go to a foreign country, it can be difficult to understand signs and notices. Here are some typical signs and notices in English. Match them with these places.

1. __l__ a restaurant
2. ___ a gas station
3. ___ a broken vending machine
4. ___ a highway
5. ___ an airport
6. ___ an automatic teller machine (ATM)
7. ___ a supermarket
8. ___ a park
9. ___ a zoo
10. ___ a hotel
11. ___ a museum
12. ___ an airplane
13. ___ a city street

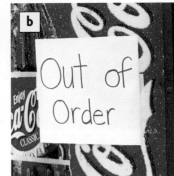

2 **T 11.5** Listen to five conversations. Where are the people?

3 Work with a partner. Choose two other places from the list in Exercise 1 above, and write brief conversations that could happen there. Read them to the class, and see if they can guess the place.

12 Dreams and reality

Second conditional · *might* · Phrasal verbs · Social expressions 2

STARTER

1 Which famous person would you like to meet? What would you talk about?

2 Which country would you like to visit? What would you do there?

3 If you had a lot of money, what would you buy? How much would you give to friends?

SWEET DREAMS
Second conditional

1 Read about Nicole. Which text describes her life? Which describes her dreams?

I live in an apartment with my Mom and my little brother. My Mom works in a hospital, so my Grandma takes care of us and helps my Mom. We have a parakeet. I go to Jefferson Elementary School, and I usually wear jeans. I can only have ice cream on Saturdays.

Nicole, age 7

If I were a princess, I'd live in a _____ . I'd have _____ to take care of me. My Mom would be queen, and she wouldn't work. I wouldn't go to school. I'd have a private _____ . I'd ride a white _____ , and I'd wear a long _____ . I could have all the _____ I wanted.

2 Complete the text on the right with these words.

| horse   ice cream   palace   dress   teacher   servants |

T 12.1 Listen and check. Then listen and repeat.

3 Look at the questions and short answers.

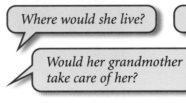

Where would she live?   *In a palace.*

Would her grandmother take care of her?   *No, she wouldn't. She'd have servants.*

Work with a partner. Ask and answer questions about Nicole's dreams.

- What ... her mother do?
- ... work?
- ... Nicole go to school?

- What pet ... have?
- What ... wear?
- ... eat a lot of ice cream?

PRACTICE

Discussing grammar

1 Make sentences from the chart.

If I	found	ice cream,	I'd	feel better.
	were	the answer,		play basketball.
	knew	a car,		lose weight.
	had	taller,	I wouldn't	buy a big house.
	didn't eat	so much,		build more hospitals.
	didn't smoke	a lot of money,		keep it.
		president,		tell you.
		some money in the street,		give you a lift.

2 Put the verbs in the correct form.

1. If I __were__ (be) rich, I __'d travel__ (travel) around the world. First I _____ (go) to Australia, then I _____ (go) to India.

2. If he _____ (work) harder, he _____ (have) more money.

3. I _____ (go) to work if I _____ (feel) better, but I feel terrible.

4. If I _____ (can) speak perfect English, I _____ (not be) in this classroom.

5. What _____ you _____ (do) if a stranger _____ (give) you $1 million?

What would you do?

3 Discuss what you would do if …
- you came home and found a burglar.

> *What would you do if you came home and found a burglar?*

> *I'd scream and run out of the house.*

- someone gave you a present that you really didn't like.
- you saw someone shoplifting.
- you found a wallet with a lot of money in it.
- you saw two people fighting in the street.

If I were you …

4 **T 12.2** We can give advice using *If I were you, I'd …*

> *I feel terrible! My head hurts, and I feel dizzy.*

> *If I were you, I'd go to bed.*

Work with a partner. Give the people advice about their problems.

1. I don't have any money.
2. My hair looks awful.
3. I have a toothache.
4. I had a fight with my boyfriend/girlfriend.
5. My car won't start in the morning.
6. My neighbors make a lot of noise.

T 12.3 Listen and compare your answers.

WHO KNOWS?
might

1 **T 12.4** Listen to two students saying what they are going to do when they graduate from college. Complete the texts.

RUTH

I _____ a vacation in Mexico for a couple of weeks, and stay in a beachfront hotel in Acapulco. Then I _____ for a job. I want to work in media—advertising or journalism would be perfect.

My sister and I _____ an apartment together, so we'll have to start looking soon. I'm very excited about the future. And I'm also very ambitious!

2 What are some of the certainties in Ruth's life?
I'm going to take a vacation in Mexico.
- … beachfront hotel in Acapulco.
- … for a job.
- … apartment together.

3 What are some of the possibilities in Henry's life?
He might go to California.
- … in a restaurant for a while.
- … in Paris.
- … a French woman …

HENRY

I'm not sure yet. Some friends have invited me to go to San Francisco with them, so I might go to California. I'll have to earn some money, so I _____ in a restaurant for a while.

I don't know what I want to do. I love France, so I _____ in Paris for a while. I could make some money painting portraits in Montmartre. Who knows? I _____ a beautiful French woman and fall in love! Wouldn't that be wonderful!

GRAMMAR SPOT

1 *Might* means the same as *Maybe ... will ...* .
What are you doing tonight?
I don't know. I might go out, or I might stay home.

2 *Might* is a modal auxiliary.
Ann might come over tonight.
I might not pass the test.
Do we add *-s* with *he/she/it*?
Do we use *do/does* in the negative?

▶▶ **Grammar Reference 12.2 p. 151**

PRACTICE

Discussing grammar

1 Choose the correct verb form.
   1. "What's for dinner?" *"We're having / We might have* roast beef. It's in the oven."
   2. "What time are we eating?" "Don't worry. *It'll be / it might be* ready before your TV program."
   3. "Who's coming to dinner?" "I invited Carlos, but *he'll be / he might be* a little late. It depends on the traffic."
   4. I'm going into town tomorrow. *I'm having / I might have* lunch with Pat at 1:00.
   5. "Are you going to take a vacation this summer?" *"I am / I might.* I haven't decided yet."

Possibilities

2 Make conversations with a partner about these future possibilities. One of you isn't sure about anything.

> *What are you doing tonight?*

> *I'm not sure. I might go out or I might stay home.*

   1. What kind/car/buy?
      Ford/Toyota.
   2. Where/on vacation?
      Thailand/Hawaii.
   3. What/have to eat?
      steak/fish
   4. Who/going to the library with?
      Tony/Robyn

3 Ask and answer questions with a partner about your possible future plans:
   • after class   • this weekend
   • this evening   • for your next vacation

Check it

4 Correct the sentences.
   1. If I'd have a car, I'd give you a lift.
   2. They'll name their baby Olivia, but they aren't sure yet.
   3. I'd visit you more often if you wouldn't live so far away.
   4. I'm playing tennis tomorrow. I'm not sure.
   5. If I'm younger, I'll learn to play the piano, but I'm too old now.

READING AND LISTENING
Ghost stories

1 Do you believe in ghosts? What would you do if you saw a ghost? Would you talk to it? Would you run away?

2 You are going to read about a man named John Roberts. He is a ghostbuster.

Do you think he ...?
- believes or doesn't believe in ghosts?
- tries to find ghosts?
- tries to get rid of ghosts?

Read the text on page 95 and find out.

3 Are the statements below true (✓) or false (✗)? Correct the false ones.

1. Mr. Roberts is a social worker.
2. He helps to work out problems for both people and ghosts.
3. He is sure that ghosts exist.
4. The boy knew it was his great-grandfather sitting on the end of his bed.
5. The old man made the boy laugh.
6. Mr. Roberts solved the boy's problem easily.
7. Ghosts are not usually members of the family.
8. Mr. Roberts says you should never talk firmly to ghosts.

4 **T 12.5** Look at the newspaper extract on the right, and then listen to an interview with Alice Lester.

Check that you know these words.

> brain scan   consultant   tumor   operation

5 Answer the questions.
1. Did Alice Lester know she had a medical problem before she heard the voices?
2. What was she doing when she first heard the voices?
3. What did the first voice tell her?
4. What happened while she was away on a trip?
5. What happened when she returned home?
6. Did the consultant believe what she told him at first?
7. What did the voices finally tell her? How is she now?

What do you think?

- Do you think Alice Lester's story is a ghost story?
- Do you believe that Mr. Roberts really gets rid of ghosts?

Telling stories

Do you know any ghost stories? In small groups, tell your ghost stories. Which is the most frightening?

Woman heard "voices" telling her of tumor
by Mark Lipman

The mysterious case of Alice Lester appeared in a leading medical journal. Alice claims that she heard voices in her head which correctly told her that she had a brain tumor.

"I'M A **GHOSTBUSTER,**" SAYS CLERGYMAN

John Roberts, 79, used to be a clergyman. He's retired now, but he still works as a ghostbuster. He helps people who have ghosts in their houses to get rid of them.

"I'm a kind of social worker for ghosts," he explains. "Some people die and they still have problems when they leave this world, so they come back again as ghosts to work them out. I don't think ghosts *might* exist, I know they *do* exist."

He says he has met thousands of ghosts trapped between this world and the next. He helps them work out their problems so they can move on to the next world.

One example is typical. At exactly nine every night a three-year-old boy got out of bed and came downstairs. When his parents asked him to explain why, he said that he saw an old man in a funny hat sitting on the end of the bed. The old man told him to get out of his bed and go downstairs.

For Mr. Roberts this was an easy problem to deal with. He moved the boy's bed from one part of the room to another. "The ghost was the boy's great-grandfather and the bed was in his way," he explains. The family was never troubled again.

"Most of the time the ghosts are members of the family. I tell people that if they want me to get rid of them, I might be throwing their grandmother out of the house. I worry that they might miss her."

Mr. Roberts calls ghosts "yesterday's people." His advice is simple. "You just need to tell them, firmly, to go away and leave you alone."

VOCABULARY
Phrasal verbs

Go away and leave me alone.

1 Phrasal verbs consist of a verb + adverb/preposition. Some phrasal verbs are literal.

Go away and leave me alone.
Take off your coat and ***sit down.***

Complete the sentences with a word from the box.

out (x2)   up   on   back

Take off your coat and sit down.

1. Put _____ something warm. It's cold today.
2. I never get _____ of bed before 8:00 on Saturdays.
3. I forgot my cell phone. Let's go _____ to the house and get it.
4. I'm going to take the dog _____ for a walk.
5. Why are your clothes on the floor? Please pick them _____ .

Do or mime these actions.

turn around   walk out   try something on   throw something away
look for something   turn something off   stand up   lie down

2 Some phrasal verbs aren't literal.

The plane ***took off.***   I ***gave up*** my job.

Do or mime these actions.

The plane took off.

put out a cigarette   look up a word   ask somebody out
run out of milk   my car broke down   Look out!   fill out a form

I gave up my job.

3 Look at the position of the object when it is a pronoun (*it, them*) in these sentences.

Your shoes are dirty. Take ***them*** *off.*   *This sweater looks nice. Can I try* ***it*** *on?*

Complete the sentences with phrasal verbs from Exercises 1 and 2. Use pronouns.

1. "Where's my tea?" "I'm sorry. I threw _____ . It was cold."
2. You shouldn't smoke that cigarette in here. Put _____ .
3. We don't need all these lights on. Turn _____ .
4. "What does this word mean?" "I don't know, but you can look _____ ."
5. I don't have time to complete this form. I'll fill _____ later.

Your shoes are dirty. Take them off.

4 Complete the sentences with one of these phrasal verbs in the correct form.

grow up   go out with   stay up   get along with   look forward to

1. How do you _____ your parents?
2. Do you like to _____ late?
3. What are you _____ doing on your next vacation?
4. Are you _____ anyone at the moment?
5. Where did you _____ ? Or have you always lived here?

In pairs, ask and answer the questions about you.

This sweater looks nice. Can I try it on?

EVERYDAY ENGLISH
Social expressions 2

1 Complete the conversations with the correct expressions.

I'm sorry.   Excuse me!   of course.   Pardon me?

1. **A** <u>Excuse me</u> ! Can I get past?
   B _____ ?
   A Can I get past, please?
   B _____ . I didn't hear you. Yes, _____ .
   A Thanks a lot.

That's right,   Oh, what a shame!   Congratulations!   Don't worry.   I hear

2. **A** _____ you're going to get married soon. _____ !
   B _____ , next July. July 21. Can you come to the wedding?
   A July 21? _____ ! That's when I'm away on vacation.
   B _____ . We'll send you some pictures.
   A That's very nice of you.

Hurry up,   all right.   Uh-oh!   Just a minute!   I have no idea.

3. **A** _____ ! Look at the time! _____ , or we'll miss the train.
   B _____ ! I can't find my umbrella. Do you know where it is?
   A _____ . But you won't need it. It's a beautiful day. Just look at the sky!
   B Oh, _____ . I'm ready. Let's go.

Good luck   See you later.   Same to you.   Good idea.   What about you?
No, of course not.

4. **A** _____ on your exam!
   B _____ . I hope we both pass.
   A Did you go out last night?
   B _____ . I went to bed early. _____ ?
   A Me, too. _____ . After the exam, let's go out for coffee.
   B _____ .

2 **T 12.6** Listen and check. Practice the conversations with a partner.

13 Making a living

Present Perfect Continuous · Word formation · Adverbs · Telephoning

STARTER

1 Ask and answer these questions.
2 Ask your teacher the same questions about *teaching* English.

> *How long have you been studying English?*

> *When did you start?*

STREET LIFE
Present Perfect Continuous

1 Read Andy's story.

2 Match the questions on page 99 with Andy's answers.

T 13.1 Listen and check. Finish Andy's answer in Question 4.

3 With a partner, cover the questions and practice the conversation. Then cover the answers, and practice again.

GRAMMAR SPOT

1 Look at the interview. Which questions are in the Present Perfect Continuous? What are the other tenses?

2 Look at these two questions.
   How long have you been selling *Street News*?
   How many copies have you sold today?
   Which question asks about a continuing activity?
   Which question asks about an action that is completed?

3 Complete these sentences with the Present Perfect Simple or Present Perfect Continuous.
   I _____ (read) this book for the past week.
   I _____ (read) two newspapers today.

▶▶ **Grammar Reference 13.1 p. 152**

STREET LIFE

ANDY'S STORY

Andy, 28, from a small town in Pennsylvania, used to have his own delivery business. When he lost his job, he also lost his home and his family. He now sleeps on the streets in New York. *Street News* is a newspaper sold by homeless people in New York. Selling newspapers gives them a small income, so they can begin to find somewhere to live.

1. ☐ _____ _____?
   For a year. It was very cold at first, but you get used to it.

2. ☐ _____ _____?
   I came here to look for work, and I never left.

3. ☐ _____ _____?
   For six months. I'm outside the subway station seven days a week selling the paper.

4. ☐ _____ _____?
   Lots. But I can't stand it when people think I drink or take drugs. My problem is I'm homeless. I want a job, but I need somewhere to live before I can get a job. So I need money to get somewhere to live, but...
   _____

5. ☐ _____ _____?
   Usually about 50.

6. ☐ _____ _____?
   So far, ten. But it's still early.

a. How many copies do you sell a day?

b. How long have you been selling *Street News*?

c. Have you made many friends?

d. How many copies have you sold today?

e. How long have you been sleeping on the streets?

f. Why did you come to New York?

4 Make more questions about Andy.

1. How long/trying to find a job?
   How long have you been trying to find a job?
2. How many jobs/had?
3. How long/standing here today?
4. How/lose your job?
5. How long/had your dog?
6. Who/best friend?
7. Where/meet him?
8. How long/known each other?

T 13.2 Listen and check.

5 Ask and answer the questions with a partner. Invent Andy's answers.

T 13.3 Listen and compare your answers.

PRACTICE

Discussing grammar

1 Choose the correct tense.

1. How long *have you been living* / *do you live* in Montreal?
2. Anna *has been finding* / *has found* a good job.
3. Pete and I *have gone out* / *have been going out* for over six months.
4. I *bought* / *have bought* a new home a few months ago.
5. How long *have you had* / *have you been having* your car?
6. Tom *worked* / *has been working* at the post office for the past month.
7. I've *written* / *'ve been writing* an essay all day.
8. I've *written* / *been writing* six pages.

Talking about you

2 Put the verbs in the Present Perfect Simple or Present Perfect Continuous or the Past Simple.

1. How long _____ you _____ (come) to this school?
2. How long _____ you _____ (use) *American Headway 2*?
3. Which textbook _____ you _____ (have) before this one?
4. How long _____ you _____ (know) your teacher?

Answer the questions about you.

What have they been doing?

3 Make a sentence about the people in the pictures using an idea from the box. Add *because* and say what they've been doing.

a. He's hot because he's been running.

hot	back hurts	paint on her clothes
tired	dirty hands	no money
wet	red face	eyes hurt

4 Complete these sentences in the Present Perfect Simple about some of the people in Exercise 3.

1. They _____ (spend) all their money.
2. She _____ (read) five books today.
3. They _____ (play) six games today.
4. He _____ just _____ (make) a cake and a pie.

Information gap

5 Work with a partner. You will each have different information about the life and career of Steven Spielberg, the movie director. Ask and answer questions to complete the information.

Student A Go to page 124.
Student B Go to page 126.

VOCABULARY
Word formation

1 These words appeared in the last few units. Complete the charts and mark the stress.

Noun	Verb
death	_die_
complaint	_____
_____	be'lieve
_____	'advertise
'promise	_____
_____	feel
ad'vice	_____
_____	de'scribe
in'vention	_____
'government	_____

Noun	Adjective
death	_____
_____	'honest
va'riety	_____
_____	suc'cessful
health	_____
_____	'beautiful
_____	'wealthy
noise	_____
_____	'comfortable
peace	_____

2 Complete the sentences with one of the words from Exercise 1.

1. **Promise** me that you'll always love me.
2. She was taken to the hospital by ambulance, but she was _____ on arrival.
3. "Are they _____ ?" "Yes, they're millionaires."
   "Where does their money come from?" "They have a very _____ business."
4. I love the _____ and quiet of the countryside.
5. I saw an _____ for a job as a waiter.
6. The sofa was so _____ that I fell asleep.
7. I gave the police a _____ of the man who attacked me.
8. I had a few problems, but Hee-Young gave me some good _____ .
9. I was sitting at home when suddenly I had a funny _____ that I wasn't alone.

Adverbs

1 Complete the sentences with the adverbs.

mainly   possibly   really   nearly

1. "Are you going out?" "_____ . I don't know yet."
2. The homework was _____ difficult. I couldn't do any of it.
3. "How old are you?" "I'm _____ eight. My birthday is next week."
4. I travel a lot in my job, _____ to Canada.

2 Complete the sentences with the adverbs.

seriously   exactly   carefully   fluently

1. I used to speak Chinese _____ , but I've forgotten it now.
2. Please drive _____ . The roads are so dangerous.
3. I have _____ $7.52 to last until the end of the week.
4. There was an accident, but fortunately no one was _____ injured.

READING AND SPEAKING

A funny way to make a living

1 As a class or in groups, play the alphabet game with jobs. Think of a job for each letter of the alphabet.

architect … businessperson …

2 What is considered to be a good job in your country? What's an average salary?

3 Look at the pictures and the headlines, and look at the three texts for ten seconds only. Answer the questions.

1. Do they have regular jobs?
2. Do they like their jobs?
3. Each headline contains one of these words. What's the difference?

> life   lively   living

4 Choose one of the texts, and read it more carefully. Answer the questions.

1. Does he/she work indoors or outdoors?
2. How long has he/she been doing this job?
3. What does he/she do in his/her job?
4. What did he/she do before?
5. Does he/she do the same thing every day?
6. How much money does he/she make?
7. Why does he/she like the job?

5 Find two partners who read the other two texts. Compare the three people. Now answer the questions.

1. Who earns the most?
2. Who earns the least?
3. What kinds of things has Terry found?
4. Why does the supermarket employ older people?
5. How long has Cathy been flying balloons?
6. What is Terry's philosophy on life?
7. Why didn't Tom call when he saw the advertisement?
8. How many hours a day does Cathy work?

What do you think?

What is your idea of the best and worst jobs in the world?

Language work

Find five adverbs that end in *-ly* in the text about the beachcomber on page 103.

Lively Tom, 69,
skates for supermarket

He gets paid for putting on his roller skates

Tom Henderson is one of 1,200 over-65s working for a supermarket chain. He's been working at his local store for 15 months, and he makes $8.00 an hour. Before that he was a plumber for 30 years.

Tom skates about five miles a day around the store grabbing things for customers who realize that they've forgotten something only when they've reached the checkout stand.

"I just love the job. I help the customers, so they're usually very nice to me. I've always liked meeting people. And it keeps me in shape. I can't sit at home doing nothing. I'd just die. I have to keep busy. Time goes really quickly. Every day is different."

The supermarket made the decision to employ people of all ages. It sees the advantages of older workers who are calmer and more authoritative when they are dealing with customers.

"When I saw this job advertised, I didn't believe they'd give it to me," says Tom. "I went in to see them in person because I thought they would be put off by my age if I just called. I wanted them to see that I am very lively for my age."

Life's a beach
Is it possible to make a living from what you can find on the beach?

For 25 years Terry Cemm was a police officer, but for the last 17 years he has been walking up and down 5 miles of beach every day, looking for things that might be useful to someone. Terry's a beachcomber.

Nearly everything in his beachfront cabin comes from the sea—chairs, tables, even cans of food. What's the most unusual thing he has ever found? "A keg of beer just before Christmas. That was nice," he remembers. He finds lots of bottles with messages in them, mainly from children. They all get a reply if there's an address in the bottle. Shoes? "If you find one, you'll find the other the next week," he says.

But does he really make a living? "Half a living," he replies. "I barter with a lot of things I find, and I have my police pension. But I don't actually need money. My life is rich in variety."

Terry seems to be a very happy man. "You have to find a way to live a simple, honest life. People spend all their lives chasing things they don't really need. There's so much waste."

"Some people say I'm crazy," says Terry. "But there are a lot more who'd like to do what I do. Look at me. I have everything that I could possibly want."

Flying for a living
Cathy has made a career out of her passion

Cathy Moorhead has only ever had one job. She has never wanted to do anything but be in a hot air balloon, going where the wind takes her, listening to the birds, and watching deer and small animals below her.

And she gets paid for it, about $50,000 a year. "I've been flying balloons since I was 10, and I have done it professionally for 12 years. I fly between 10 and 20 passengers in different balloons." The flights usually last an hour, and they go early in the morning or just before sunset. "The trips are always mystery tours," she says. "I never know where we're going to land."

She starts work about 6 A.M., and works anywhere from 15 hours a day to nothing, if the weather is bad. "We can't fly if it's too windy, if visibility is poor, or if it's raining. The balloon gets too heavy and the passengers get wet." What's the best thing about the job? "The job itself. I love being out in the country and I hate routines. So this is heaven for me."

LISTENING AND SPEAKING
Phoning home

1 Craig has recently moved to San Francisco and has just started his first job as a computer programmer. He's on the telephone with his mother.

> **T 13.4** Listen to his side of the conversation.

Work with a partner and decide if these statements are true (✓) or false (✗).

1. Craig starts work at eight o'clock at night.
2. His mother is worried that he hasn't been eating well.
3. He goes home immediately after work.
4. Craig's mother has not heard about Linda before.
5. Craig and Linda share an apartment.
6. Linda has been working at the software company longer than Craig.
7. Craig's father has been working in Canada.
8. Craig's father has been working hard all day.
9. His mother is going to San Francisco next Thursday.
10. Craig and Linda are going to cook dinner for his mother.

2 **T 13.4** Listen to Craig again. Your teacher will stop the recording after each of Craig's answers. What do you think his mother said?

3 **T 13.5** Listen to the complete conversation and compare your ideas.

Language work

Read the tapescript on page 137. <u>Underline</u> examples of the Present Perfect Simple and the Present Perfect Continuous.

Role play

1 Read Ruth's diary. Work with a partner. One of you is Ruth. It's Friday evening and one of you has called the other to talk.

> *Hi, there. I'm exhausted. I've had a terrible week!*

> *What have you been doing?*

2 Work with a partner. It is Friday evening. One of you has decided to call the other to talk. Ask and answer questions about what you've been doing this week.

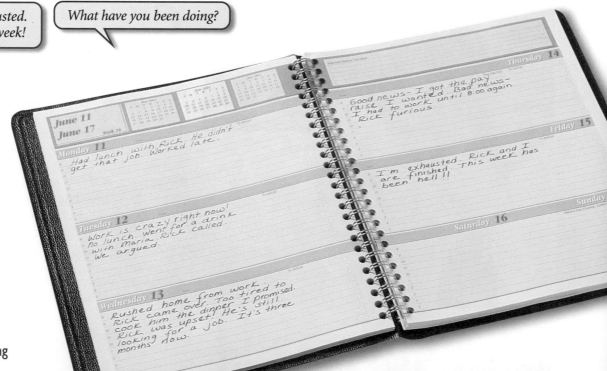

June 11 – June 17 Week 24

Monday 11
Had lunch with Rick. He didn't get that job. Worked late.

Tuesday 12
Work is crazy right now! No lunch. Went for a drink with Maria. Rick called. We argued.

Wednesday 13
Rushed home from work. Rick came over. Too tired to cook him the dinner I promised. Rick was upset. He's still looking for a job. It's three months now.

Thursday 14
Good news – I got the pay raise I wanted. Bad news – I had to work until 8:00 again. Rick furious.

Friday 15
I'm exhausted. Rick and I are finished. This week has been hell!!

Saturday 16

Sunday

EVERYDAY ENGLISH
Telephoning

1 Practice saying these telephone numbers.

(919) 677-1303 (212) 726-6389 (847) 432-5655
555-1212 (800) 451-7556

T 13.6 Listen and check.

2 **T 13.7** Listen to some phone numbers in British English. What differences are there between American English and British English?

3 **T 13.8** Listen to three phone conversations and decide:

Who is speaking to who?	What are they talking about?	How well do they know each other?
1.		
2.		
3.		

> **!**
>
> **1** Look at these telephone expressions.
>
> Hello?
> Who's calling? / Who's speaking? / Who's this?
> This is John. (NOT ~~Here is~~ John, or ~~I'm~~ John.)
>
> **2** Complete these expressions from the telephone conversations.
>
> Could I _____ Ann Baker?
> I'm sorry, but Mike's _____ right now.
> Can I take _____ ?
> I'll _____ later.
>
> **3** What do these expressions mean?
>
> *One moment, please.*
> *Speaking.*

4 Look at the tapescript on page 138. Practice the conversations with a partner.

5 Work in pairs. You are each going to make a phone call.

Student A Go to page 125.
Student B Go to page 127.
Student C Go to page 125.
Student D Go to page 127.
Student E Go to page 125.
Student F Go to page 127.

14 All you need is love

STARTER ▶ Match the lines about John and Mary.

They met each other	every week.
They've known each other	when they met.
They see each other	for a long time.
They were living in Seattle	a long time ago.
They had never been to Seattle	before.

A LOVE STORY
Past Perfect

1 Texts A and B are summaries of a magazine love story. Read and compare them.

One Short H⊙t Summer
by Carmen Day

A *The story so far ...*
Saskia met Brad at a party one Saturday night in June. They fell in love and got married the following Saturday. After the wedding, Brad moved into Saskia's apartment. Saskia called her parents and told them that she was married. They were furious.

Unfortunately, after a few months, Brad began to behave very strangely and his marriage to Saskia started to go wrong ...

B *The story so far ...*
Saskia and Brad got married one Saturday in June. They had met only one week earlier at a party and had fallen in love. After the wedding, Saskia called her parents and told them that she was married, and that Brad had moved into her apartment. They were furious.

Unfortunately, after a few months, their marriage started to go wrong. Brad had begun to behave very strangely ...

GRAMMAR SPOT

1 Which text tells the events of the story in chronological order (= the order that they happened)? What tense are *all* the verbs in this text?

2 How is the following idea expressed in Text B?
They met at a party and fell in love.
Which two tenses are used in Text B?

3 What's the difference between these sentences?

When we arrived	they were leaving.
	they left.
	they had left.

▶▶ **Grammar Reference 14.1 p. 152**

2 **T 14.1** Read and listen to Text B on page 106 and <u>underline</u> all the examples of the Past Perfect. Read the text aloud and pay attention to contracted forms.

3 Are the following statements about Saskia and Brad true (✓) or false (✗)? Correct the false ones.

1. When Saskia and Brad got married, they had known each other for a year.
2. When Saskia told her parents about the wedding, Brad had moved into her apartment.
3. Her parents were angry because she hadn't called them for a long time.
4. The marriage started to go wrong, and then Brad began to behave very strangely.

PRACTICE

Speaking

1 The story continues. Work with a partner. Tell the story in the order of the pictures.

1. On Friday evening when Brad returned from work, he … his suitcase.

2. Then he …

3. and …

4. Saskia … home.

2 Which of these sentences is true? Explain why.

When Saskia arrived home, Brad	was packing.
	packed.
	had packed.

3 Tell the story again, but begin at Picture 4.
When Saskia arrived home, Brad had packed …

4 Make sentences from the chart below.

I	was a mess			had	hurt it playing soccer.
Our teacher	was sore				done the homework.
My leg	died		I		passed all my exams.
The plants	was delighted	because			had a party the night before.
The house	was angry		we		forgotten to water them.
	was hungry			hadn't	had a busy day.
	went to bed early				had any breakfast.

T 14.2 Listen and check. Practice saying the sentences.

5 The *had* in the Past Perfect tense is often contracted.

I'd passed my exams. (The *'d* is sometimes difficult to hear.)

(*'d* is also the contracted form of *would*: *I'd like to come.*)

T 14.3 Listen to the sentences. Put a check (✓) if the sentence contains *had*.

1. ☐   3. ☐   5. ☐   7. ☐   9. ☐
2. ☐   4. ☐   6. ☐   8. ☐   10. ☐

6 Put the verbs into the correct tense, Past Simple or Past Perfect.

The story continues ...

Saskia (1) _____ (read) Brad's letter and then she (2) _____ (walk) slowly into the kitchen.

Earlier that day she (3) _____ (buy) his favorite food for dinner; now she (4) _____ (throw) it into the trash can. Why (5) _____ he _____ (do) this to her? She remembered how happy they (6) _____ (be) in the beginning. They (7) _____ (laugh) a lot then. Saskia (8) _____ (feel) desperate.

One hour later the phone (9) _____ (ring) in the apartment ...

7 Read the end of the story. What happened before? Write your ideas in groups.

The end of the story

Brad took Saskia in his arms and said, "Forgive me, my darling. I'm so happy we're together again—this time it's forever!"

WHAT DID SHE SAY?
Reported statements

1 **T 14.4** What does Mary say about John? Listen and complete the sentences.

A	What does Mary say?
"I _____ John very much."	
"We _____ six months ago."	
"I _____ in love before."	
"We _____ very happy."	
"I _____ him forever."	
"I _____ him this evening."	

2 **T 14.5** Read and listen to the sentences below.

B	What did Mary tell you?
She told me that / She said that ...	
she loved John very much.	
they had met six months ago.	
she had never been in love before.	
they were very happy.	
she would love him forever.	
she was seeing him that evening.	

GRAMMAR SPOT

1 **A** is direct speech. **B** is reported speech. What are the tense changes from direct to reported speech?

2 How are *say* and *tell* used to introduce reported speech?

▶▶ **Grammar Reference 14.2 p. 152**

---

3 Practice the sentences using contracted forms where possible.

She told me that she'd met him six months ago.

PRACTICE

An interview

1 **T 14.6** Listen to an interview with the writer Carmen Day, who wrote *One Short Hot Summer*.

2 Complete this report of the interview with the correct verb forms.

Carmen Day – romance novelist

In an interview Carmen said she (1) __had written__ another romantic novel because she (2) _____ romantic fiction easy to write, but that her next novel (3) _____ something different, possibly a detective story.

Carmen said that the character of Brad (4) _____ on her first husband, Charles Ford, the actor, who (5) _____ her very unhappy. But she added that she (6) _____ now married to Tony Marsh, who is a lawyer. She said that they (7) _____ married for nearly ten years and that they (8) _____ extremely happy together.

She told me that she (9) _____ now _____ five novels, and also that she (10) _____ three stories for children. She said she (11) _____ never stop writing, not even when she (12) _____ an old lady.

T 14.7 Listen and check.

Check it

3 Report these statements.
1. "I like Ana," said Jim.
2. "I'm staying with my aunt," said Ana.
3. "Mr. Lee called before lunch," Sue said.
   "He didn't leave a message," she added.
4. "I don't think it'll rain," said Ken.
5. "Ken's gone home," Sue said.
   "He went early," she added.
6. "I'll call you tonight," Ana told Jim.

READING AND SPEAKING
The tale of two silent brothers

1 Sometimes in families there are arguments and family members don't speak to each other for a long time. Has this ever happened to anyone you know?

2 You are going to read about two brothers who didn't speak to each other for many years. These expressions are in the text. Match the verbs and phrases.

get	a bachelor all his life
make	a coin
have	revenge
see	a will
remain	an argument
toss	and make up
kiss	a lawyer about something

3 Read the first part of the story.

PART ONE | A death in the family

There were once two brothers, John and Robert Hessian. John was 52 years old, Robert 49. They had never married and they lived together in a large house. They lived together, they ate meals together, but they never spoke a single word to each other. They hadn't spoken to each other for ten years, ever since they had had an argument. Whenever they wanted to communicate, they wrote notes.

One evening the brothers were sitting together after dinner. They were both wearing black because their older sister, Mary, had recently died. John wrote a note to Robert: *Mr. Liversage is coming to visit.* (Mr. Liversage was their lawyer.) Robert wrote: *Why?*
John wrote: *I don't know. He called and said that he wanted to see us.*
At that moment there was a knock at the door. It was the lawyer, Mr. Powell Liversage. He had gone to school with the brothers and was an old friend. He too was unmarried.
"How are you, Powell?" asked Robert.
"Very well," he replied. "I've come to tell you about your sister's will. Did you know that she had left a will?"
"No," answered John and Robert together. "How much did she leave?"
"$25,000. But let me read you the will."

What do you think?

Discuss these questions with a partner before you read Part Two.

Why do you think the brothers argued? Do you think they argued about:

- money? • the house? • a woman?

What do you think is in the will? Do you think:

- the sister leaves the brothers $12,500 each?
- she leaves all the money to one brother? Which one?
- she leaves them the money on certain conditions? What conditions?

4 Read Part Two and find out if your ideas are correct.

PART TWO | The will

Mr. Liversage took the will out of his pocket and began to read.

Last Will and Testament of Mary Hessian

To my dear brothers John and Robert:

You have both behaved very stupidly. I have never understood why you argued about Annie Emery. You have been cruel and unfair to poor Annie. She has waited ten years for one of you. So, John, if you marry Annie, I'll give all my money to you. And Robert, if you marry her, I'll give it to you. And, if neither of you marries her, all my money will go to Annie, herself.

Your ever-loving sister,

Mary

What do you think?

Discuss these questions as a class before you read Part Three.

- What do you think will happen?
- What will John and Robert do?
- Who will marry Annie?

5 Read Part Three and find out if your ideas are correct.

PART THREE | To marry or not to marry?

The two brothers sat and thought for a long time. Ten years ago when Annie was a young woman of 27, both John and Robert had been in love with her. They had had a violent argument and some terrible things were said. Afterward they had both wanted to make up and be friends again but by this time they had stopped speaking to each other, so neither of them learned that the other had decided not to marry Annie.

At two o'clock in the morning John spoke: "Why don't we toss a coin for Annie? Heads or tails?"

"Tails," said Robert. But it was heads. The next evening John went over to Annie's house. Powell Liversage was just leaving when he arrived.

So in the end neither brother married Annie. They are still bachelors to this day, but at least they are now talking to each other again. And Annie? Well, she got her revenge and now she's very happily married.

ADAPTED FROM A STORY BY ARNOLD BENNETT

What do you think?

Discuss these questions with a partner. Then tell the class your ideas.

- What happened when John went to Annie's house?
- Why didn't Annie marry either brother?
- Who did she marry?
- Who got the money?

See page 123 to find out what actually happened.

Language work

Complete the sentences using the Past Perfect.

1. John and Robert didn't speak to each other
   because they had had an argument.
2. They were wearing black because …
3. They didn't know that their sister …
4. Mary said in her will that …
5. When Annie was 27, both brothers …
6. Annie told John that she wouldn't marry him or his brother because …

LISTENING AND VOCABULARY
Talk to me

1 **T 14.8** Close your books and your eyes and listen to a song. What is it about?

2 Work with a partner. Complete the song, choosing the best word for each line from the box.

Talk to Me by Bruce Springsteen

Well, every night I see a _____ up in your window

But every night you won't _____ the door

But although you won't _____ let me in

From the street I can see your _____ sitting close to him

light	man
come to	answer
never	ever
silhouette	shadow

What must I do?
What does it take
To get you to

Talk to me
Until the night is over
Talk to me
Well until the night is over, yeah yeah yeah
I got a full week's _____
And baby I've been working hard _____ day
I'm not _____ for the world, you see
I'm just asking, girl
Talk to me

pay	stay
all	each
asking	looking

Well late at night I hear music that
    you're playing _____ and low
Yes and late at night I see the two of
    you _____ , so close
I don't understand darling, what was
    my _____?
Why am I down here below _____
    you're up there with him?

soft	loud
sitting	swaying
mistake	sin
while	when

What did I do?
What did I say?
What must I pay
To get you to
Talk to me

3 **T 14.8** Listen again and check.

EVERYDAY ENGLISH
Saying good-bye

1 Match the sentences with the correct photos.

1. __c__ "Good-bye! Have a safe trip. Send us a postcard!"
2. ___ "Good-bye. Thank you for a wonderful evening. You'll have to come over to our place next time."
3. ___ "Good-bye. It's been very interesting talking to you. We'll let you know in the next week or so."
4. ___ "Bye! Have a nice weekend."
5. ___ "Bye-bye! Thank you for inviting me to the party."
6. ___ "Good-bye. Here's my number. Just call me if you have any problems with it."
7. ___ "Good-bye! Drive carefully and call us when you get there!"
8. ___ "Good-bye! Good luck in the future. I've really enjoyed our classes together!"

2 **T 14.9** Listen and check. Practice saying the sentences.

3 Make more conversations for these situations:
- parents saying good-bye to son/daughter going away to college
- saying good-bye to friends after spending a vacation with them
- saying good-bye to your teacher/boss after finishing school/work on Friday
- saying good-bye to teachers/classmates when the semester is over

Getting Information

PRACTICE

Getting information

Ask and answer questions to complete the information about Judy Dandridge.

Student A When did she start working as a mail carrier?
Student B Twenty years ago, when she was twenty-two.
Why does she drive a truck?
Student A Because she delivers mail long distances to people who live in the country.
What time … ?

Judy Dandridge

Judy Dandridge started working as a mail carrier _20 years ago, when she_ _was 22_ (*When?*). She drives a truck because she delivers mail long distances to people who live in the country, far from towns and cities.

She gets up at _____ (*What time?*) and starts work at 5:00. Every day she drives about _____ miles (*How many miles?*). She finishes work at 2:00 in the afternoon.

After work she goes _____ (*Where?*) and has lunch with her husband, Jim. He works _____ (*Where?*). They like gardening, so they often spend the afternoon outside in their garden.

They have two teenage children. Last year Judy, Jim, and the kids went to _____ (*Where?*) and visited Jim's sister. They stayed for _____ (*How long?*).

They're going to Florida next month because _____ (*Why?*). It's Judy's parents' wedding anniversary, and they want everyone to be there.

PRACTICE

Getting information

1 Ask Student B questions about Mike and Nicole to complete your chart.

Name	Town and country	Family	Occupation	Free time/ vacation	Present activity
Mike				• •	
Lucy	London, England	a son and a daughter	part-time teacher	• reading, going to the movies • Florida	drinking tea
Nicole				• •	
Jeff and **Wendy**	Melbourne, Australia	one daughter and three grandchildren	• He works in an office. • She is a hairdresser	• tennis, swimming • Bali every summer	having a barbecue in the backyard

2 Use your chart to answer Student B's questions about Lucy and Jeff and Wendy.

Mike

Lucy

Nicole

Jeff and Wendy

PRACTICE
Getting information

Work together to complete the information about Judy Dandridge.
Ask and answer questions.

Student A When did she start working as a mail carrier?
Student B Twenty years ago, when she was twenty-two.
Why does she drive a truck?
Student A Because she delivers mail long distances to people who live in the country.
What time … ?

Judy Dandridge

Judy Dandridge started working as a mail carrier 20 years ago, when she was 22. She drives a truck because _she delivers mail long distances to people who live in the country far from town and cities_ (*Why?*).

She gets up at 3:30 in the morning and starts work at _____ (*When?*). Every day she drives about 75 miles. She finishes work at _____ (*What time?*).

After work she goes home and has lunch with _____ (*Who / with?*). He works in a grocery store. They like _____ (*What / like doing?*), so they often spend the afternoon outside in their garden.

They have _____ (*How many?*) teenage children. Last year Judy, Jim, and the kids went to Los Angeles and visited _____ (*Who?*). They stayed for ten days.

They're going _____ (*Where?*) next month because their family is having a big party. _____ (*Why?*)

PRACTICE
Getting information

1 Use your chart to answer Student A's questions about Mike and Nicole.

Name	Town and country	Family	Occupation	Free time/ vacation	Present activity
Mike	Vancouver, British Columbia, Canada	a sister	works for computer company	• skiing, playing ice hockey • Mexico	playing ice hockey
Lucy				• •	
Nicole	Dallas, Texas, the United States	two brothers and a dog!	high school student	• listening to music • Europe	getting ready to go out
Jeff and **Wendy**				• •	

2 Ask Student A questions about Lucy and Jeff and Wendy to complete your chart.

UNIT 1, page 6

Student A

READING
Communication

1 Read the list of messages below. Can you communicate them without using any words? Mime each idea for Student B. He/she must guess what you are trying to communicate.

- What time is it?
- Do you want a cup of coffee?
- I have a headache.
- I'm hot/cold.
- I like your haircut.
- I can't carry this bag.

2 Student B will try to mime some messages. Can you guess what he/she is trying to communicate?

UNIT 3, page 21

Student A

PRACTICE
Getting information

Ask and answer questions to complete the text.

Student A When did Mr. and Mrs. Harman arrive home?
Student B At 10:30 in the evening.
Where was Sue staying?
Student A She was staying with friends.
Why … ?

After the party

Mr. and Mrs. Harman arrived home __at 10:30 in the evening__ (*When?*). Sue was staying with friends. She felt _____ (*How?*) because her parents would be furious with her.

Her parents started to _____ (*What?*). Then they phoned Sue and told her _____ (*What?*).

Sue got back home at 2:00 in the morning. She said _____ (*What?*), and she promised that she would never have another party.

PRACTICE

Comparing four capital cities

1 Read about Washington, D.C., and Tokyo.

WASHINGTON, D.C.		
Founded	1791	
Population	606,900	
Area	16,863 km2	
Temperatures	Jan: 3°C	July: 26°C
Rainfall	Jan: 69mm	July: 97mm
Km from the sea	150	

TOKYO		
Founded	1456	
Population	12 million	
Area	16,808 km2	
Temperatures	Jan: -4°C	July: 26°C
Rainfall	Jan: 3mm	July: 192mm
Km from the sea	180	

2 Ask Student B these questions to find out about Stockholm and Brasilia. Complete the charts below.

- How old is it?
- How big is it?
- How many people live there?
- How hot/cold does it get?
- How wet is it?
- How far is it from the sea?

Student A How old is Stockholm?
Student B It's very old. It was founded in …

STOCKHOLM		
Founded	_____	
Population	_____	
Area	_____	
Temperatures	Jan: _____	July: _____
Rainfall	Jan: _____	July: _____
Km from the sea	_____	

BRASILIA		
Founded	_____	
Population	_____	
Area	_____	
Temperatures	Jan: _____	July: _____
Rainfall	Jan: _____	July: _____
Km from the sea	_____	

3 Use the information in Exercise 1 to answer Student B's questions about Washington, D.C., and Tokyo.

4 Now compare the four cities.

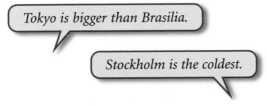

Tokyo is bigger than Brasilia.

Stockholm is the coldest.

5 Compare some cities in your country.

READING
Communication

1 Student A will try to mime some messages. Can you guess what he/she is trying to communicate?

2 Read the list of messages below. Can you communicate them without using any words? Mime each idea for Student A. He/she must guess what you are trying to communicate.

- I'm tired.
- Can you swim?
- Do you have any money?
- This food is too hot.
- I'll call you at 7:00.
- What's that awful smell?

PRACTICE
Getting information

Ask and answer questions to complete the text.

Student A When did Mr. and Mrs. Harman arrive home?
Student B At 10:30 in the evening.
Where was Sue staying?
Student A She was staying with friends.
Why … ?

After the party

Mr. and Mrs. Harman arrived home at 10:30 in the evening. Sue was staying _____with friends_____ (*Where?*). She felt terrible because _____ (*Why?*).

Her parents started to clean the house. Then they phoned _____ (*Who?*) and told her to come home immediately.

Sue got back home at _____ (*What time?*). She said she was very sorry, and she promised _____ (*What?*).

PRACTICE

Comparing four capital cities

1 Read about Stockholm and Brasilia.

STOCKHOLM		
Founded	1250	
Population	692,954	
Area	6,488 km2	
Temperatures	Jan: -3°C	July: 18°C
Rainfall	Jan: 43mm	July: 61mm
Km from the sea	0	

BRASILIA		
Founded	1960	
Population	492,500	
Area	5,814 km2	
Temperatures	Jan: 20°C	July: 19°C
Rainfall	Jan: 94mm	July: 46mm
Km from the sea	600	

2 Use the information in Exercise 1 to answer Student A's questions about Stockholm and Brasilia.

Student A How old is Stockholm?
Student B It's very old. It was founded in …

3 Ask Student A these questions to find out about Washington, D.C., and Tokyo. Complete the charts below.

- How old is it?
- How big is it?
- How many people live there?
- How hot/cold does it get?
- How wet is it?
- How far is it from the sea?

WASHINGTON, D.C.		
Founded	_____	
Population	_____	
Area	_____	
Temperatures	Jan: _____	July: _____
Rainfall	Jan: _____	July: _____
Km from the sea	_____	

TOKYO		
Founded	_____	
Population	_____	
Area	_____	
Temperatures	Jan: _____	July: _____
Rainfall	Jan: _____	July: _____
Km from the sea	_____	

4 Now compare the four cities.

Tokyo is bigger than Brasilia.

Stockholm is the coldest.

5 Compare some cities in your country.

PRACTICE
Find someone who...

1 What number did you choose on page 51? Match that number to one of the sentences below.

1. Find someone who has been to California.
2. Find someone who has been to Europe.
3. Find someone who has been to Australia.
4. Find someone who has written a letter or e-mail in English.
5. Find someone who has been skiing.
6. Find someone who has had a party for more than 30 people.
7. Find someone who has tried Thai food.
8. Find someone who has flown in a balloon.
9. Find someone who has been horseback riding.
10. Find someone who has climbed a mountain.

11. Find someone who has won a contest.
12. Find someone who has met a famous person.
13. Find someone who has read a book by an American or Canadian author.
14. Find someone who has broken a bone.
15. Find someone who has been windsurfing.
16. Find someone who has written a poem.
17. Find someone who has been in a car accident.
18. Find someone who has lost something important.
19. Find someone who has worked on a farm.
20. Find someone who has **never** failed an exam.

2 Use the information in your sentence to make a question, beginning
Have you ever ... ?

Have you ever been to California?

3 Stand up, and ask your classmates your question.
When someone answers "Yes, I have," ask questions to find out more.

Have you ever been to California? *Yes, I have.*

What did you do there? *Where did you go?* *How long were you there?*

What were the people like? *Did you enjoy it?*

3 Report back to the class.

No one has been to California. *Paulo and Sonia have been to California. They ...*

UNIT 9, page 70

READING AND SPEAKING
What do you think?

According to official statistics, here are the ten largest cities in the world:

1.	Tokyo-Yokohama, Japan	29,971,000
2.	Mexico City, Mexico	27,872,000
3.	São Paulo, Brazil	25,354,000
4.	Seoul, South Korea	21,976,000
5.	Mumbai, India	15,357,000
6.	New York City, the United States	14,648,000
7.	Osaka-Kobe-Kyoto, Japan	14,287,000
8.	Tehran, Iran	14,251,000
9.	Rio de Janeiro, Brazil	14,169,000
10.	Kolkata, India	14,088,000

Source: US Census Bureau, 2000

UNIT 14, page 111

Reading and Speaking
What do you think?

What actually happened

Annie refuses to marry either of the brothers because they treated her so badly and behaved so stupidly by not talking to each other. She married the lawyer, Mr. Powell Liversage, but she did not keep the $25,000 that Mary left her. She gave it to John and Robert to share.

PRACTICE
Getting information

Ask and answer questions to complete the information about Steven Spielberg.

Student A Where was he born?
Student B He was born in Ohio.
How much has he earned in his career?
Student A Millions of dollars.
How long … ?

Steven Spielberg

Steven Spielberg was born _____in Ohio_____ (*Where?*). He is one of the most successful filmmakers in recent times, and in his career he has earned millions of dollars. He has been making movies since _____ (*How long?*) when he made a war movie, *Escape to Nowhere*. He was only 13. He studied English Literature at California State University and then worked _____ (*Where?*) for seven years.

In 1975, he made the movie *Jaws*, which was very successful, and made him rich and famous. Since then, he has made more than 30 movies, including the box-office hits *Close Encounters of the Third Kind*, *Indiana Jones*, *ET*, and *Jurassic Park*. He has also directed more serious movies, like _____ (*Which movies?*), and he has produced a lot of hit movies. In 1994, he formed _____ (*What?*). Recently, Dreamworks has been working with Microsoft to produce interactive computer games and videos.

EVERYDAY ENGLISH
Role play

1 Read your role.

- Be sure you understand the situation.
- What decisions will you make?

STUDENT A	STUDENT C	STUDENT E
Situation You're at home. It's 7:00 in the evening. You're watching TV. You've already done your homework. It was the vocabulary exercise on page 101 of *American Headway Student Book 2*. **Decision** What are you doing for the rest of the evening? Going out? Staying in? **The phone call** A friend who's in the same class as you, is going to call. When the phone rings, pick it up and say hello.	**Situation** You're American. You live in a large American city. You're at home. It's 7:00 in the evening. Today is the 18th. Next week, on the 25th, a foreign student is coming to stay at your house while he studies English for a month at a nearby university. You don't know what time he is arriving at the airport. The airport is about 30 miles (about 48 km) from your home. **Decision** Are you going to meet him at the airport? Or will he want to come into the city by taxi or bus? If he takes the airport bus, will he come directly to your home or will you meet him at the bus station? **The phone call** The student is going to call you. When the phone rings, pick it up and say hello. Ask questions such as "How are you?," "Have you packed yet?" At the end of the conversation, say "We're looking forward to meeting you."	**Situation** You're at home in your apartment, which you share with a roommate. It's 7:00 in the evening. Your roommate is out right now. **Decision** Where is your roommate? When will he/she be back? Do you know what he/she's doing tonight, or not? **The phone call** Someone is going to call. When the phone rings, pick it up and say hello. If it's for your roommate, say "Can I take a message?"

2 Find a partner.

Student A Find a Student B.
Student C Find a Student D.
Student E Find a Student F.

Role-play a phone conversation with your partner. Start the conversation.

3 Act out your phone conversation for the class.

PRACTICE
Getting information

Ask and answer questions to complete the information about Steven Spielberg.

Student A Where was he born?
Student B He was born in Ohio.
How much has he earned in his career?
Student A Millions of dollars.
How long ... ?

Steven Spielberg

Steven Spielberg was born in Ohio. He is one of the most successful filmmakers in recent times, and in his career he has earned _____millions of dollars_____ (*How much?*). He has been making movies since 1961 when he made a war movie, *Escape to Nowhere*. He was only 13. He studied _____ (*What?*) at California State University and then worked in the television division at Universal Studios in Hollywood for seven years.

In 1975, he made the movie *Jaws*, which was very successful, and made him rich and famous. Since then, he has made _____ (*How many?*) movies, including the box-office hits *Close Encounters of the Third Kind*, *Indiana Jones*, *ET*, and *Jurassic Park*. He has also directed more serious movies, like *Schindler's List* and *Saving Private Ryan*, and he has produced _____ (*How many hit movies?*). In 1994, he formed a new Hollywood studio, Dreamworks. Recently, Dreamworks has been working with _____ (*Who _____ with?*) to produce interactive computer games and videos.

EVERYDAY ENGLISH
Role play

1 Read your role.

- Be sure you understand the situation.
- What decisions will you make?

STUDENT B	STUDENT D	STUDENT F
Situation You're at home. It's 7:00 in the evening. It's time to do tonight's English homework, but you have a problem. You've forgotten what the homework is, and you left your copy of *American Headway Student Book 2* at school. You're going to call a friend who's in the same class. **Decision** What are you doing for the rest of the evening? If you need to borrow a copy of *American Headway Student Book 2* could you go over to your friend's house? What time? **The phone call** Call your friend. **A** will start the conversation. Ask "How are you?" and talk a little before you ask about the homework. Say "I've forgotten what tonight's homework is. Do you know?"	**Situation** You come from a country where English is not the main language. Today is the 18th. Next week, on the 25th, you're flying to the United States for a month to study English at a university. You're going to stay with an American family. They live in a large city, but you don't know their exact street address. You're going to call them to tell them what time you expect to arrive. **Decision** What time does the plane arrive? Do you want the family to meet you or will you take a bus or taxi from the airport? If you are going to take a bus, you need to know how to get from the bus station to their home. If you take a taxi, you need directions for the driver. **The phone call** Call the family. They will start the conversation. Say "I'm calling to tell you when my flight arrives." Don't forget to ask for the address.	**Situation** It's 7:00 in the evening. You want to talk to a friend of yours. It's very important— you've found a used car that you think he/she'd like to buy. **Decision** If he/she isn't home, are you going to leave a message? Are you going to call again later, or do you want your friend to call you back? Will you be at home for the rest of the evening, or are you going out? **The phone call** Call your friend. The other person starts the conversation.

2 Find a partner.

Student B   Find a Student A
Student D   Find a Student C
Student F   Find a Student E

Role-play a phone conversation with your partner. Let your partner start the conversation.

3 Act out your phone conversation for the class.

Tapescripts

Unit 1

T 1.1 Mauricio

My name's Mauricio Nesta. I come from Brasilia, the capital of Brazil. I'm a student at the University of Brasilia. I'm studying modern languages—English and French. I also know a little Spanish, so I can speak four languages. I'm enjoying the program a lot, but it's really hard work. I started college three years ago.

I live at home with my parents and my sister. My brother went to work in the United States last year.

After I graduate, I'm going to work as a translator. I hope so, anyway.

T 1.2 Carly

Hi. My name's Carly and I come from Toronto, but I live near Boston now with my husband, Dave, and our three children. Dave's an architect. I came to the US 15 years ago when I got married.

I work part-time in a bookstore. I'm also taking courses on the Internet. It's called "virtual university." I study at home, on my computer, and I send my work in by e-mail every week. I'm studying art. It's really interesting and I'm enjoying the program a lot. But it isn't easy having a part-time job and studying, too! Right now, I'm reading about Italian painters in Italian, which is difficult because I speak French quite well but only a little Italian!

I started the program a year ago and it lasts for three years. After I graduate, I'm going to look for a job in an art gallery or museum.

T 1.3

1. I'm reading a good book.
   I booked a room at a hotel.
2. What kind of music do you like?
   My mother is a very kind person.
3. Can you swim?
   I'd like a can of soda, please.
4. What does *architect* mean?
   Don't be mean to your little sister!
5. Please turn on the light.
   This box is very light.
6. Do you want to play tennis?
   We saw a play at the theater.
7. The train's coming.
   Athletes have to train very hard.
8. The phone's ringing.
   What a beautiful ring you're wearing!

T 1.4 Mrs. Snell

I have a new neighbor. He moved in a few weeks ago. I know he has a job, because I see him leaving the house every morning and then coming home in the evening. He's a construction worker, I think. He wears jeans and a T-shirt, so it can't be a very good job. Sometimes he comes home late.

One time he knocked on my door, but I didn't open it. I didn't know who it was, and I don't like to open my door to strangers. So, I've never actually met him and I don't know what I would say to him, anyway. Kids these days. They're so different now!

You know his girlfriend is living with him. I know it's not unusual these days, but I still don't like it, boys and girls living together and not married. It's such a small apartment. I don't know how two people can live there.

He had a party last week. Forty people! The noise! It went on until two in the morning. I didn't sleep all night. He said he was sorry the next day, but it was a little bit late by then.

Oh, there he goes. I can see him now. He's going out with his girlfriend. I wonder what they're doing tonight. Having a good time. Going to a club, probably.

T 1.5 Steve

I moved into this apartment a few weeks ago, and I'm really enjoying living here. There's only one bedroom, and my sister is staying with me right now because she's looking for a job.

I work in advertising. It's hard work, and the hours are really long, but I like it. And it pays well. The office is really casual. No one wears a suit or a tie.

My neighbors are all really nice. I've met them all except Mrs. Snell, I think that's her name. She's very quiet. I never see her or hear her. I knocked on her door once to introduce myself, but she didn't answer. She doesn't like young people or something, I don't know.

I had a party a few days ago. It really wasn't very noisy. About ten of us were here at my place until 11:00 and then we went out to a club. When I saw Mrs. Snell the next day, I said I hoped there wasn't too much noise, but as usual she didn't say anything. She's really odd.

This evening my sister and I are going to visit a friend of ours who's in the hospital, and then we're going out for Chinese food.

T 1.6 Social expressions

1. "How are you?" "Fine, thanks."
2. "Hello, Jane!" "Hi, Peter!"
3. "See you tomorrow!" "Bye! See you then."
4. "Good night!" "Sleep well!"
5. "Good morning!" "Good morning!"
6. "Hello, I'm Elaine Paul." "Nice to meet you, Elaine."
7. "Cheers!" "Cheers!"
8. "Excuse me." "Yes. Can I help you?"
9. "Make yourself at home." "Thank you. That's very nice of you."
10. "Have a good weekend!" "Same to you!"
11. "Thank you very much." "You're welcome."
12. "Bless you!" "Thanks."

Unit 2

T 2.1 Three countries

d. Well, my country's got a population of uhh … about three and a half million, so it's not a big place. Most of the people are from Europe, but about 12 percent are Maori … they were the original inhabitants. A lot of people live in bungalows, which are small houses on one floor, and have a pet. It's a very beautiful country. It's got a lot of mountains, and people love the countryside. Oh, and we're very good at rugby and cricket.

e. My country is the biggest island in Europe, but we have less than 1 percent of the world's population, fewer than 60 million. Most people live in cities and towns, but we've got a beautiful, green countryside, because of all the rain we get. We're famous for drinking tea in the afternoon, and we like to socialize at pubs in the evening, maybe have a pint or two of beer. A favorite hobby is gardening, and our top sports are cricket, rugby, and football—or soccer, as the Americans call it.

f. I come from a big country. It has a lot of wide open spaces. We have a population of … oh … about 280 million. We have big, cosmopolitan cities with people who come from all over the world. But lots of people live in the suburbs and in smaller cities and towns. We're famous for hamburgers and french fries, but we have other kinds of food, too. In fact, you can find almost any kind of food you want here. We like sports—baseball, basketball, and, of course, football!

T 2.2 See p. 12

T 2.3 Questions

Where does he come from?
Is she married?
Do they have any children?
How many brothers and sisters does she have?
What does he do?
What does she do in her free time?
Where do they go on vacation?
What is she doing right now?

T 2.4 Daily life

have breakfast
wash my hair
watch a movie on TV
talk to my friends

take a shower
clean up the mess
do the dishes
have or put posters on the wall

make some coffee
listen to music
relax on the sofa
do my homework

cook a meal
go to the bathroom
put on makeup
read magazines

P = Presenter   C = Carol   M = Mike
D = Dave   A = Alison

P Hello, and welcome to "Home Truths." Today we're going to hear just what couples really think of each other. What drives you crazy about your partner? Here's Carol, talking about her husband, Mike.

C Well, there are a lot of arguments about television in our house. He gets hold of the remote control and then he's always changing channels, so I never see what I want to. All he wants to watch is sports, sports, sports. When I try to talk to him, he doesn't listen because he's watching the TV. And … another thing … he never remembers anything—birthdays, when we're going out, nothing. Oh, and he can't make a decision to save his life. I have to do it all. I decide where we're going on vacation, what car to buy, which restaurant when we go out for dinner … everything.

P So there we have Carol's opinion. What does Mike say about Carol?

M When we're in the car and I'm driving, she constantly tells me how to drive. She'll say "you're going too fast," or "slow down," or give me directions like "make a left turn here," even though I know exactly where I'm going and don't need any help. And then, when I want to watch something on television, like … the news, she always wants to watch a talk show or a movie. And … another thing. She's always on the phone. She spends hours talking to our daughter, and do you know where she lives? Right around the corner.

P But what do they think of their marriage? Here's Carol.

C Well, I can't change him now, so I'll just have to put up with him.

P And Mike?

M We've been married for 25 years, and she's the only woman for me!

P And now we have another couple, Dave and Alison. Oh, and by the way, Dave's an electrician.

A What drives me absolutely crazy is that he starts a job and never finishes it. At work he's so professional, but at home, if I ask him to change a lightbulb in the bedroom, it takes him months. And he's so messy. I tried to train him before we got married, but it didn't work. He just drops things on the floor. I keep saying that I don't want to be his mother as well as his wife. When we go out, he looks so scruffy, even when I'm all dressed up. And his clothes are so old-fashioned. He never throws anything away.

P Oh, boy. Now what does Dave have to say about Alison?

D Well, she's never ready on time. She always finds something to do that makes us late, wherever we go. She's usually doing her hair or putting on her makeup while I'm saying "Come on, honey, it's time to go." And she forgets things. She forgets where she parked the car, she leaves the car keys in the most stupid places. But the most annoying thing about Alison is that she's always right!

P And their final opinions about each other?

A He's great. He's a lot of fun, and he's one in a million.

D See? I told you, she's always right!

P So, there we are. My thanks to Carol and Mike, and Dave and Alison.

J = Jim   M = Maria
1. **J** Hello. What's your name?
   M Maria.
   J I'm … Jim. I'm a teacher. And … where are you from?
   M Rome.
   J Uhh … What … what do you do?
   M I'm a student.
   J Mm. And … how long have you been here in Seattle, Maria?
   M Two months.
   J Are you having a good time?
   M Yes.
   J Can I get you a coffee?
   M No.
   J Do miss your family at all?
   M No.
   J Do you have any brothers or sisters?
   M Yes.
   J Umm … Oh! What do they do?
   M They are students, too.
   J Oh, well, I have a class now. Good-bye, Maria.
   M Ciao.

A = Alice   M = Sergio
2. **A** Hello. What's your name?
   M Sergio. And what's your name?
   A Alice. Where are you from, Sergio?
   M I come from Rio de Janeiro in Brazil, one of the most beautiful places in the whole world. And you, Alice, where do you come from?
   A I come from Canada. What do you do in Rio?
   M I'm an architect.
   A Oh, really?
   M Yeah. I design beautiful buildings for people with lots of money. I'm very expensive.
   A How interesting.
   M And how long have you been a teacher, Alicia?
   A Actually, my name's Alice.
   M I am so sorry. Alicia is the way we say it in Brazil—Alice, I mean.
   A Don't worry. I like the name Alicia. I've been working here for five years.
   M How interesting! Do you enjoy it?
   A Yes, very much. You meet a lot of people from lots of different countries, and I like that very much. Are you enjoying it here?
   M Very, very much. I'm learning a lot of English, I'm making a lot of friends, and even the weather's not so bad! Well, I haven't frozen to death yet, and I've been here for five weeks. Alice, can I get you a coffee?
   A Well, I've got a few minutes before my next class, so that would be nice. Thank you very much …
   M Why don't we …

1. What a nice day it is today!
   Yes. It's beautiful, isn't it?
2. How are you today?
   Fine, thanks. How about you?
3. Did you have a nice weekend?
   Yes, we had a great time. We went to the beach and did some shopping.
4. How do you like living in Texas?
   I'm enjoying it. It was kind of strange at first, but I'm getting used to it.
5. Did you have a good flight?
   Yes, no problems. The plane was a little bit late, but it didn't matter.
6. Did you watch the soccer game yesterday?
   No, I missed it. What was the score?
7. What a beautiful coat you're wearing!
   Thank you. I got it in San Francisco last year.

Unit 3

 see p. 18

1. Russell woke up at two o'clock.
2. He woke up because he was thirsty.
3. He heard a noise in the kitchen.
4. He found three men.
5. Russell's mother kept her wallet in her bedroom.
6. They left at five o'clock.
7. When they left, Russell watched TV.
8. The police caught the burglars yesterday.

a. asked
   showed
   wanted
   walked
   started
b. tried
   carried
c. liked
   believed
   used
d. stopped
   planned

1. I broke a cup, but I fixed it with glue.
2. I felt sick, so I went to bed.
3. I made a sandwich because I was hungry.
4. I took a shower and washed my hair.
5. I lost my passport, but then I found it in the back of a drawer.
6. I called the police because I heard a strange noise.
7. I ran out of coffee, so I bought some more.
8. I forgot her birthday, so I said I was sorry.
9. The phone rang, so I answered it.
10. I told a joke but nobody laughed.

Hands up, I've Got a Burger!
Last Tuesday a man armed with just a hot hamburger in a bag stole $1,000 from a bank in Danville, California.

Police Detective Bill McGinnis said that the robber, who was wearing a mask, entered the Mount Diablo National Bank at about 1:30 P.M. and gave the teller a note demanding $1,000. He claimed that he had a bomb in the bag. The teller said she could smell a distinct odor of hamburger coming from the bag. Even so, she handed the money to the man. As he was running out of the bank, he dropped the bag with the hamburger. He escaped in a car that was waiting for him outside.

Teenage Party Ends in Tears

When Jack and Kelly Harman went away on vacation, they left their teenage daughter alone in the house. Sue, aged 16, wanted to stay at home because she was studying for a test. Her parents said she could have some friends stay over. However, Sue decided to have a party. Everyone was having a good time when suddenly things started to go wrong. Forty uninvited guests arrived, and some of them were carrying knives. They broke furniture, smashed windows, and stole jewelry. When Mr. and Mrs. Harman heard the news, they came home immediately.

T 3.6 **A spy story—*The Man with the Golden Gun***

James Bond got back to his hotel room at midnight. The windows were closed and the air conditioner was on. Bond switched it off and opened the windows. His heart was still thumping in his chest. He breathed in the air with relief, then he took a shower and went to bed.

At 3:30 he was dreaming, not very peacefully, about three black-coated men with red eyes and angry white teeth. Suddenly he woke up. He listened. There was a noise. It was coming from the window. Someone was moving behind the curtain. James Bond took his gun from under his pillow, got quietly out of bed, and crept slowly along the wall toward the window. Someone was breathing behind the curtain. Bond pulled it back with one quick movement. Golden hair shone in the moonlight.

"Mary Goodnight!" Bond exclaimed. "What are *you* doing here?"

"Quick, James! Help me in!" Mary whispered urgently.

Bond put down his gun and tried to pull her through the open window. At the last moment the window banged shut with a noise like a gunshot.

"I'm really sorry, James!" Mary Goodnight whispered.

"Shh! Shh!" said Bond. He quickly led her across the room to the bathroom. First he turned on the light, then the shower. They sat down on the side of the bathtub.

"Mary," Bond asked again. "What on earth are you doing here? What's the matter?"

"James, I was so worried. An urgent message came from HQ this evening. A top KGB man, using the name Hendriks, is staying in this hotel. He knows you're here. He's looking for you!"

"I know," said Bond. "Hendriks is here all right. So is a gunman named Scaramanga. Mary, did HQ say if they have a description of me?"

"No, they don't. They just have your name, Secret Agent James Bond."

"Thanks, Mary. Now, I have to get you out of here. Don't worry about me. Just tell HQ that you gave me the message, OK?"

"OK, James." Mary Goodnight stood up and looked into his eyes. "Please be careful, James."

"Sure, sure." Bond turned off the shower and opened the bathroom door. "Now, come on!"

Suddenly a voice came from the darkness of the bedroom. "This is not your lucky day, Mr. Bond. Come here, both of you, and put your hands up!"

Scaramanga walked to the door and turned on the lights. His golden gun was pointing directly at James Bond.

T 3.7 **Dates**

January eighth, nineteen ninety-eight
July sixteenth, nineteen eighty-five
November twenty-fifth, two thousand two

T 3.8 **Dates**

the eighth of January, nineteen ninety-eight
January the eighth, nineteen ninety-eight
the sixteenth of July, nineteen eighty-five
July the sixteenth, nineteen eighty-five
the twenty-fifth of November, two thousand and two
November the twenty-fifth, two thousand and two

T 3.9 **Dates**

June nineteenth
August fifth
July fourth
March first
February third
January twenty-first, nineteen eighty-eight
December second, nineteen ninety-six
April fifth, nineteen eighty
June eleventh, nineteen sixty-five
October eighteenth, two thousand
January thirty-first, two thousand five

Unit 4

T 4.1 see p. 26

T 4.2 see p. 27

T 4.3 ***something/someone/somewhere***

1. Did you meet anyone nice at the party?
   Yes. I met someone who knows you!
2. Ouch! There's something in my eye!
   Let me look. No, I can't see anything.
3. Let's go somewhere nice for our vacation.
   But we can't go anywhere that's too expensive.
4. I'm so unhappy. Nobody loves me.
   I know somebody who loves you. Me.
5. I lost my glasses. I looked everywhere, but I couldn't find them.
6. Did you buy anything when you were shopping?
   No, nothing. I didn't have any money.
7. I'm bored. I want something interesting to read, or someone interesting to talk to, or somewhere interesting to go.
8. It was a great party. Everyone loved it.

T 4.4 see p. 29

T 4.5 **Buying things**

1. A Hello. Can I help you?
   B I'm just looking, thanks.
   …
   B I'm looking for a sweater like this, but in blue. Do you have one?
   A I'll take a look. What size are you?
   B Medium.
   …
   A Here you are.
   B That's great. Can I try it on?
   A Of course. The fitting rooms are over there.
   …
   B I like it.
   A It fits you very well.
   B How much is it?

A $59.99.
   B OK. I'll take it.
   A How would you like to pay?
   B Cash.
2. A Hi. I wonder if you could help me. I have a bad cold and a sore throat. Can you give me something for it?
   B OK. You can take these twice a day.
   A Thank you. Could I have some tissues too, please?
   B Sure. Anything else?
   A No, that's all. Thanks.
   B OK. That's $8.35.
3. A Could you help me? I'm looking for this month's issue of *Vogue*. Can you tell me where it is?
   B Right there on the middle rack. Next to *Latina*.
   A Thanks.
   B That's $3.50.
4. A Good morning. Can I have a black coffee, please?
   B With sugar?
   A No, thanks. Oh, and a doughnut, please.
   B I'm sorry, but there aren't any left. We have some delicious muffins.
   A I'll have a blueberry muffin.
   B Will that be all today?
   A That's it.
   B That'll be $2.75, please.
   A OK.

T 4.6 **Everyday conversations**

1. A A book of stamps, please.
   B That'll be six dollars.
2. A How much is this sweater?
   B Twenty-eight fifty.
3. A A loaf of sourdough bread and three rolls, please.
   B That'll be two dollars and eighty-two cents.
4. A Just this book, please.
   B All right. Let's see … . Where's the price? Ah! That's five ninety-five.
5. A How much was your car?
   B Fifteen thousand dollars.
6. A How much was the check for?
   B A hundred and sixty pounds.

Unit 5

T 5.1

Duane
When I grow up, I want to be a basketball player and play for the Los Angeles Lakers, because I want to make a lot of money. After that, I'm going to be an astronaut, and fly in a rocket to Mars and Jupiter. And I'd like all the people in the world and all the animals in the world to be happy.

Maria
I just finished my second year of college, and now I'm going to take a year off. My friend and I are going around the world. We hope to find work as we go. I really want to meet people from all over the world, and see how different people live their lives.

Jim
What I'd really like to do, because I'm crazy about planes and everything about flying, is to have my own business connected with planes, something like a flying school. I'm getting married next June, so I can't do anything about

it yet, but I'm going to start looking this time next year.

Martin
My great passion is writing. I write plays. Two have been performed already, one in Toronto and one in a small, off-Broadway theater in New York. But my secret ambition … and this would be the best thing in my life … I would love to have one of my plays performed on Broadway. That would be fantastic.

Amy
We're thinking of moving, because the kids will be leaving home soon. Meg's 18, she's a high school senior this year, so with any luck, she'll be going off to college next year. And Kate's 15. Jack and I both enjoy walking, and Jack likes fishing, so we're going to move to the country.

Helen
Well, I broke my arm recently, so what I really want to do is to go back to the health club as soon as possible. I really enjoy swimming. At my age, it's important to stay in shape, and I want to be able to travel without feeling sick. I'm going to retire in a couple of years, and I'm looking forward to having more time to do the things I want to do.

T 5.2 **Complete the questions**

1. **A** I hope to go to college.
   B What do you want to study?
   A Math.
2. **A** One of my favorite hobbies is cooking.
   B What do you like to make?
   A Soups, salads, everything.
3. **A** I get terrible headaches.
   B When did you start getting them?
   A About two years ago.
4. **A** We're planning our vacation now.
   B Where are you thinking of going?
   A Peru.
5. **A** I'm tired.
   B What would you like to do tonight?
   A Just stay home and watch TV.

T 5.3 **Listen and check**

1. **A** What are the guys doing this afternoon?
   B They're going to watch a baseball game. The Chicago Cubs are playing.
2. **A** Darn it! I dropped one.
   B I'll pick it up for you.
   A Thank you. That's very nice of you.
3. **A** What's Sue doing next year?
   B She's going to travel around the world.
   A Lucky her!
4. **A** The phone's ringing.
   B Oh, I'll answer it. I'm expecting a call.
5. **A** I don't have any money.
   B Don't worry. I'll lend you some.
   A Thanks. I'll pay you back tomorrow. I won't forget.
6. **A** What are you and Pete doing tonight?
   B We're going out for dinner. It's my birthday.

T 5.4 **Complete the conversation**

1. "My bag is so heavy." "Give it to me. …"
2. "I bought some warm boots because …"
3. "Tony's back from vacation." "He is? …"
4. What are you doing tonight?
5. Are you coming to our class party?

6. Congratulations! I hear …
7. I need to mail these letters.
8. Where are you going on your vacation this year?

T 5.5 **"You've Got a Friend"**

When you're down and troubled
And you need a helping hand
And nothing, but nothing is going right
Close your eyes and think of me
And soon I will be there
To brighten up even your darkest nights.
Chorus
You just call out my name,
and you know wherever I am
I'll come running to see you again.
Winter, spring, summer, or fall
All you have to do is call
And I'll be there, yeah, yeah, yeah,
You've got a friend.
If the sky above you
Turns dark and full of clouds
And that old north wind begins to blow
Keep your head together
And call my name out loud
And soon I'll be knocking on your door.
Hey, ain't it good to know that you've got a friend?
People can be so cold.
They'll hurt you and desert you.
Well, they'll take your soul if you let them.
Oh, yeah, but don't you let them.
(Chorus)

T 5.6 **How do you feel?**

1. "I feel nervous. I have a test today." "Good luck! Do your best."
2. "I don't feel very well. I think I'm getting the flu." "Why don't you go home and go to bed?"
3. "I'm feeling a lot better, thanks. I have a lot more energy." "That's good. I'm glad to hear it."
4. "I'm really excited. I'm going on vacation to Bangkok tomorrow." "That's great. Have a good time."
5. "I'm sick of this weather. It's so wet and miserable." "I know. We really need some sun."
6. "I'm really tired. I didn't sleep very well last night." "That happens to me sometimes. I just read in bed."
7. "I'm kind of worried. My grandfather's going into the hospital for tests." "I'm sorry to hear that, but I'm sure he'll be all right."
8. "I feel really depressed right now. Nothing's going right in my life." "Cheer up! Things can't be that bad!"

Unit 6

T 6.1 **Todd's tennis tour**

T = Todd   E = Ellen
E You're so lucky, Todd. You travel all over the world. I never leave Chicago!
T Yeah, but it's hard work. I just practice, practice, practice, and play tennis all the time. I don't get time to see much.
E What about last year? Where did you go? Tell me about it.

T Well … in January I was in Melbourne, for the Australian Open. It's a beautiful city, kind of big and very cosmopolitan, like Chicago. There's a nice mixture of old and new buildings. January's their summer, so it was hot when I was there.
E And what's Dubai like? When were you there?
T In February. We went from Australia to Dubai for the Dubai Tennis Open. *Phew!* Boy, is Dubai hot! Hot, very dry, very modern. Lots of really modern buildings, white buildings. Interesting place, I enjoyed it.
E And Paris?! That's where I want to go! What's Paris like?
T Everything that you imagine! Very beautiful, wonderful old buildings but lots of interesting modern ones, too. And of course very, very romantic, especially in May. Maybe I can take you there sometime.
E Yeah?

T 6.2 **What's Chicago like?**

T = Todd   F = Todd's friend
F What's the weather like?
T Well, Chicago's called "the windy city" and it really can be windy!
F What are the people like?
T They're very interesting. You meet people from all over the world.
E What are the buildings like?
T A lot of them are very, very tall. The Sears Tower is 110 stories high.
F What are the restaurants like?
T They're very good. You can find food from every country in the world.
F What's the nightlife like?
T Oh, it's wonderful. There's lots to do in Chicago.

T 6.3 ***Big, Bigger, Biggest!***

Melbourne was interesting, but for me, Paris was more interesting than Melbourne, and in some ways Dubai was the most interesting of all because it was so different from any other place I know. It was also the hottest, driest, and most modern. It was hot in Melbourne but not as hot as in Dubai. Dubai was much hotter! Melbourne is much older than Dubai but not as old as Paris. Paris was the oldest city I visited, but it has some great modern buildings, too. It was the most romantic place. I loved it.

T 6.4 see p. 44

T 6.5 see p. 44

T 6.6 **Conversations**

1. **A** I moved to a new apartment last week.
   B Really? What's it like?
   A Well, it's bigger than my old one but it isn't as modern and it's farther from work.
2. **A** I hear Sandy and Al broke up.
   B Yeah. Sandy has a new boyfriend.
   A Really? What's he like?
   B Well, he's much nicer than Al, and much more handsome. Sandy's happier now than she's been for a long time.
3. **A** We have a new teacher.
   B Really? What's she like?
   A Well, I think she's the best teacher we've ever had. Our old teacher was good, but our new one's even better and she makes us work much harder.

4. **A** Did you get a new car?
   B Well, it's secondhand, but it's new to me.
   A What's it like?
   B Well, it's faster than my old car and more comfortable, but it's more expensive to keep up. I love it!

T 6.7 **Living in another country**

J = Jane   C = Carla

J When I say that I live in Sweden, everyone always wants to know about the seasons …
C The seasons?
J Yeah … you know how cold it is in winter, what it's like when the days are so short.
C So what *is* it like?
J Well, it *is* cold, very cold in winter, sometimes as cold as -26° Centigrade, and of course when you go out you wrap up in warm clothes, but inside, in the houses, it's always very warm.
C And what about the darkness?
J Well, yeah. Around Christmas time, in December, there's only one hour of daylight …
C One hour!?
J Uh-huh. Only *one* hour of daylight, so you really look forward to the spring. It is kind of depressing sometimes but you know, the summers are amazing. From May to July, in the north of Sweden, the sun never sets—it's still light at midnight. You can walk in the mountains and read a newspaper.
C Oh, yeah. The land of the midnight sun.
J That's right. But it's wonderful, you want to stay up all night, and the Swedes make the most of it. Often they start work earlier in summer and then leave at about two or three in the afternoon, so that they can really enjoy the long summer evenings. They like to work hard but play hard, too. I think a lot of people in the US work longer hours, but I'm not sure it's such a good thing.
C Is it hot in the summer?
J Yeah, it gets pretty warm, but it's not as hot and humid as in some American cities like New York or Washington, D.C. And Swedes don't use air conditioning as much as Americans.
C So what about free time? Weekends? Holidays? Vacations? What do Swedish people like doing?
J Well, every house in Sweden has a sauna …
C *Every* house!?
J Well, every house I've been to. And most people have a country cottage, so people like to leave the city and get back to nature on weekends. These cottages can be fairly primitive—no running water and not even toilets, and …
C No *toilet*?
J Well, *some* don't have toilets but they *all* have a sauna and everyone in the family sits in it together; then they run and jump into the lake to get cool.
C What!? Even in winter?
J Yeah. Swedish people are very healthy.
C *Brrr!* Or crazy!

T 6.8 **Synonyms**

1. "Mary's family is very rich." "Well, I knew her *uncle* was very wealthy."
2. "Look at all these new buildings!" "Yes. This city's much more modern than I expected."

3. "Wasn't that movie wonderful?" "Yes, it was great."
4. "George doesn't have much money, but he's so thoughtful." "Yes, he is. He's one of the most generous people I know."
5. "Steve and Elaine's house is huge." "Yes, it's absolutely enormous."
6. "I'm bored with this lesson!" "I know, I'm really sick of it, too!"

T 6.9 **Antonyms**

1. Mark's apartment isn't very big.
2. Paul and Sue aren't very generous.
3. This TV show isn't very interesting.
4. Their children aren't very polite.
5. John doesn't look very happy.
6. His sister isn't very smart.

T 6.10 **Directions**

You go down the path, past the pond, over the bridge, and through the gate. Then you go across the road. Take the path through the park and into the woods. When you come out of the woods, just follow the path up the steps and into the museum. It takes about five minutes or less.

Unit 7

T 7.1 **Listen and check**

1. He sang pop music and jazz. She sings jazz, pop, and rhythm & blues.
2. He recorded more than 600 songs and sold over 50 million records. She has made over 17 albums so far.
3. She was born in Los Angeles and has lived in California for most of her life. He was born in Montgomery, Alabama, grew up in Chicago, then later moved to California.
4. She has been married twice and has one son. She married for the first time in 1976. He was married twice and had five children.

T 7.2 **Listen and check**

1. Nat King Cole won many awards, including a Grammy Award in 1959 and Capitol Records' "Tower of Achievement" award. Natalie Cole has won eight Grammies and many other awards for her singing.
2. He had his own TV show in 1956 and appeared in a number of movies. She has appeared in several TV specials and TV movies.
3. She received a degree in psychology from the University of Massachusetts in 1972. She has lived mostly in California since then.
4. She has been a recording artist for more than 25 years. She recorded her first album, *Inseparable,* in 1975. With that album she won two Grammy Awards in 1976.
5. Her remarkable album, *Unforgettable with Love,* came out in 1991. On it, she sang the song "Unforgettable" as a "duet" with her father's voice. Since then, the album has sold over five million copies.

T 7.3 **What are the questions?**

1. How many albums has she made?
2. Where has she lived for most of her life?
3. How many times has she been married?
4. How many children does she have?
5. Has she won any awards for her singing?
6. What university did she go to?

7. How long has she been a recording artist?
8. When did she record her first album?

T 7.4 **for and since**

1. I've known my best friend for years. We met when we were ten.
2. I last went to a movie two weeks ago. It had Tom Cruise in it.
3. I've had this watch for three years. My dad gave it to me for my birthday.
4. We've used this book since the beginning of the semester. It's OK. I kind of like it.
5. We lived in our old apartment from 1994 to 2000. We moved because we needed a bigger place.
6. We haven't had a break for an hour. I really need a cup of coffee.
7. I last took a vacation in 1999. I went camping with some friends.
8. This building has been a school since 1989. Before that it was an office building.

T 7.5 **Asking questions**

A Where do you live, Mi-Young?
B In an apartment near the park.
A How long have you lived there?
B For three years.
A And why did you move?
B We wanted to live in a nicer area.

T 7.6 **An interview with Style**

I = Interviewer   S = Suzie   G = Gary

I … and that was the latest record from Style called "Give It to Me." And guess who is sitting right next to me in the studio? Suzie Tyler and Gary Holmes, who are the two members of Style. Welcome to the show!
S Thanks a lot. It's nice to be here.
I Now you two have been very busy this year. You've had a new album come out, and you've been on tour. How are you feeling?
S Pretty tired. We've just finished a tour of the UK, and in April we went to Japan, Taiwan, and Australia, so yeah … we've traveled a lot this year.
G But we've made a lot of friends, and we've had some fun.
I Tell us something about your background. What did you do before forming Style?
G Well, we both played with a lot of other bands before teaming up with each other.
I Who have you played with, Suzie?
S Well, over the years I've sung with Lionel Richie and Phil Collins and Bon Jovi.
I And what about you, Gary?
G I've recorded with Genesis and UB40, and I've given concerts with U2. And of course, Ace.
I Why is Ace so important to you?
G Because I had my first hit song with them. The song was called "Mean Street," and it was a hit all over the world … that was in 1995.
I So how long have you two been together as Style?
S Since 1997 … quite a few years. We met at a recording studio while I was doing some work with Bon Jovi. We started talking and Gary asked me if I'd like to work with him, and that's where it all started.
I Suzie, you're obviously the vocalist, but do you play any music yourself?

S Yes, I play keyboards.
I And what about you, Gary?
K I play guitar and harmonica. I can play the drums, but when we're doing a concert we have a back-up group.
I So where have you two traveled to?
S Well, … uhh … sometimes I think we've been everywhere, but we haven't really. We've toured in the UK, and we've been to Japan, Taiwan, and Australia, but we've never been to South America. That's the next place we'd like to go. And then Eastern Europe. I'd love to play in those places.
G You forgot Mexico. We went there two years ago.
S Oh, yeah.
I Over the years you've made a lot of recordings. Do you know exactly how many?
G That's a difficult question, umm …
I Well, about how many?
S Oh, I don't know. Maybe about 25.
G Yeah, something like that.
I And how long have you been in the music business?
G I guess about 15 years. I've never had another job. I've only ever been a musician, since I was 17.
S I've had all kinds of jobs. When I graduated from college, I worked as a waitress, a sales assistant, a painter, a gardener … I could go on and on …
I Well, stop there, because now you're a member of a band. Suzie and Gary, it was great talking to you. Good luck with the new album.
S/G Thanks.
I And now for something different. We're …

T 7.7 Word pairs

1. "Do you still play tennis?" "Not regularly. Just now and then, when I have time."
2. This is a pretty relaxed place to work. There aren't many dos and don'ts.
3. Here you are at last! I've been so worried! Thank goodness you've arrived safe and sound.
4. "Do you like your new job?" "Yes and no. The money's OK, but I don't like my boss."
5. Sometimes there are too many people in the house. I go out on the patio for some peace and quiet.
6. Good evening, ladies and gentlemen. It gives me great pleasure to talk to you all tonight.
7. "How's your grandmother?" "Up and down. There are good days, and then not such good days."
8. It's been so wet! I'm sick and tired of this rain! When will it ever stop?

T 7.8 Short answers

1. A Do you like learning English, Ana?
   B Yes.
   A Do you like learning English, Ana?
   B Yes, I do. I love it. It's the language of Shakespeare.
2. A Are those new jeans you're wearing?
   B No.
   A Are those new jeans you're wearing?
   B No, they aren't. I've had them for ages.
3. A Do you know what time it is?
   B No.
   A Do you know what time it is?
   B No, I don't. I'm sorry.

4. A Can you play any musical instruments?
   B Yes.
   A Can you play any musical instruments?
   B Yes, I can, as a matter of fact. I can play the violin.

Unit 8

T 8.1 Steve's job

I = Interviewer   S = Steve
I What kind of hours do you work, Steve?
S Well, I have to work very long hours, about 11 hours a day.
I What time do you start?
S I work nine 'til three, and then I have to start again at five-thirty and work until eleven. Six days a week. So I don't have much time for fun.
I And do you have to work on weekends?
S Oh, yes. That's our busiest time. I get Wednesdays off.
I What are some of the things you have to do, and some of the things you don't have to do?
S Well … I don't have to wash the dishes, so that's good! I have to wear white, and I have to be very careful about hygiene. Everything in the kitchen has to be totally clean.
I What's hard about the job?
S You're standing up all the time. When we're busy, people get angry and shout, but that's normal.
I How did you learn the profession?
S Well, I took a two-year course in college. In the first year we had to learn the basics, and then we had to take exams.
I Was it easy to find a job?
S I wrote to about six hotels, and one of them gave me my first job, so I didn't have to wait too long.
I And what are the secrets of being good at your job?
S Attention to detail. You have to love it. You have to be passionate about it.
I And what are your plans for the future?
S I want to have my own place. When the time is right.

T 8.2 Listen and repeat

1. I have a good job. I have to work hard.
2. He has a nice car. She has to get up early.
3. I had a good time. I had to take exams.

T 8.3 should or must

1. "I'm working 16 hours a day." "I think you should talk to your boss."
2. "I can't sleep." "You shouldn't drink coffee at night."
3. "My ex-boyfriend's getting married." "I don't think you should go to the wedding."
4. "I've had a terrible toothache for weeks." "You must go to the dentist! Don't wait!"

T 8.4 Vacations in January

Fatima
In winter the weather is wonderful. It's the perfect time of year, not too hot, not too cold, but the temperature can change a lot in just one day. It can go from fairly chilly to very warm, so you should bring a jacket but you don't need any heavy winter clothes. The capital city is the most populated city in the world and there are lots of

things to see and do there. We have lots of very old, historic buildings. We are very proud of our history, with Mayan and Aztec temples. But you should also go to the coast. We have beautiful beaches. Maybe you've heard of Acapulco.

You don't need a lot of money to enjoy your vacation. There are lots of good inexpensive hotels and restaurants, and of course you must visit the markets. You can buy all kinds of pottery and things pretty cheaply, and don't forget our wonderful fruits and vegetables. We have one hundred different kinds of pepper. You should try tacos, which are tortillas, a kind of bread, filled with meat, beans, and vegetables. And our beer is very good, especially if you add lemon and salt. Or, of course, you can always drink coffee.

Ali
It's usually mild in winter, and it doesn't often rain, so you don't have to bring warm clothes. But you'll need a light coat or a sweater because it can get cool in the evenings.

There is so much to see and do. We have some wonderful museums, especially the museum of Islamic art, and the mosques are beautiful, but of course what everyone wants to see is the Pyramids. You must visit the Pyramids. Go either early in the morning or late in the afternoon. The light is much better then. And if you have time, you should take a cruise down the Nile. That's really interesting. You can visit all kinds of places that are difficult to get to by land.

The best place to try local food is in the city center. You should try *koftas* and *kebabs*, which are made of meat, usually lamb. You should also try falafel, which is a kind of ball made of beans mixed with herbs, it's fried until it's crispy. It's delicious. One of the nicest things to drink is tea, mint tea. It's especially good if the weather is very hot, it's really refreshing.

Toni
Well, of course in January, in my country it can be very cold, with lots of snow, so you must bring lots of warm clothes, coats and woolly hats, and, if you can, snow boots.

Many people go skiing in the mountains on the weekends and when you are up so high, the sky is blue, the sun can feel quite hot. It's warm enough to even have lunch outside. But you don't have to go skiing, there are lots of other things to do and see. A lot of our towns are very pretty. They look exactly the same today as they did four hundred years ago. And we have beautiful lakes. If the weather is good, you can go for a boat trip on Lake Geneva and get really beautiful views of the mountains.

The food you must try is fondue, which is cheese melted in a pot. You put pieces of bread on long forks to get it out. It's one of our specialties and it's delicious!

T 8.5 Advice column

1. Children always need the support of their parents, whether they're 4 or 24. I think you should pay for him to get some job training, and when he's ready, you should help him find somewhere to live. Meanwhile, you have to give him all the love that he needs.
2. I decided to give it all up and change my life dramatically three years ago. Since then, I have had the most exciting three years of my life. It can be scary, but if you don't do it, you

won't know what you've missed. I don't think you should worry. Go for it.

3. He's using you. I think you should tell him to move out. It's time for him to go. Twenty-four is too old to be living with his parents. He has to take responsibility for himself. And you must tell the police about his gang activities. Sometimes you have to be cruel to be kind.

4. Why should he accept it? He isn't their slave; they don't own him. And I too can't stand the way people use their cell phones in restaurants and on trains and buses. They think that the people around them are invisible and can't hear. It is so rude.

5. I think she should be very careful before she gives up her job and goes to live abroad. Does she think that the sun will always shine? If there is something in her life that makes her unhappy now, this will follow her. She should take her time before making a decision.

6. He has to keep it! He should have a talk with his supervisor and come to an agreement. Why can't he turn it off sometimes? Cell phones are great, and if he has one for free, he's very lucky. They are one of the best inventions ever.

T 8.6 Words that go together

alarm clock	hairdryer
movie star	sunset
traffic light	earring
credit card	can opener
ice cream	bookcase
sunglasses	rush hour
coffee break	cigarette lighter
raincoat	earthquake

T 8.7 A visit to the doctor

D = doctor   M = Manuel

D Hello. Come and sit down. What seems to be the matter?
M Well, I haven't felt very well for a few days. I have a slight temperature, and I just feel terrible. I have a stomachache, too.
D Have you been feeling nauseous?
M Yes, and I've vomited a few times.
D Mmm. Let me have a look at you. Your glands aren't swollen. Do you have a sore throat?
M No, I don't.
D Have you had diarrhea at all?
M Yes, I have, as a matter of fact.
D Have you had anything to eat recently that might have disagreed with you?
M No, I don't think … Oh! I went to a barbecue a few days ago and the chicken was a little bit undercooked.
D It could be that, or just something that was left out of the refrigerator for too long.
M Yes, I started feeling sick that night.
D Well, you should get some rest, and I'll give you something for the stomachache and diarrhea. Drink plenty of liquids, and just take it easy for a while. I'll write you a prescription.
M Thank you. Can I get the prescription filled here?
D No, you have to take it to a pharmacy.
M OK. Thank you very much. Good-bye.
D Good-bye.

Unit 9

T 9.1 A year off

1. We're traveling around the world before we go to college.
2. We're going to leave as soon as we have enough money.
3. When we're in Australia, we're going to learn to scuba dive on the Great Barrier Reef.
4. If we get sick, we'll take care of each other.
5. After we leave Australia, we're going to Europe.
6. We can stay with my friends while we're in Madrid.
7. Our parents will be worried if we don't stay in touch.
8. We'll stay in Europe until we run out of money.

T 9.2 When, as soon as

1. When I get home, I'm going to take a shower.
2. As soon as this class is over, I'm going home.
3. If I win, I'll buy a new car.
4. After I finish high school, I want to go to college.
5. While I'm in New York, I'll do some shopping.
6. I'm going to travel the world before I get too old.

T 9.3 When I get to Vancouver …

Paul Bye, Honey. Have a good trip to Vancouver.
Mary Thanks. I'll call you as soon as I arrive at the hotel.
Paul OK, but remember I'm going out with Henry tonight.
Mary Well, if you're out when I call, I'll leave a message on the answering machine so you'll know that I've arrived safely.
Paul Great. What time do you expect to get there?
Mary If the plane arrives on time, I'll be at the hotel about 10:00 P.M.
Paul All right. Give me a call as soon as you know the time of your flight back, and I'll pick you up at the airport.
Mary Thanks, Hon. Don't forget to water the plants while I'm away.
Paul Don't worry. I won't forget. Bye!

T 9.4 Life in the 21st century

A So what's the name of that book you were reading? Is it any good?
B Yeah, it is. It's called Visions, by a scientist named Michio Kaku. It's about the ways that science will change how we live in this century.
A Cool. So, what's going to change?
B Lots of stuff. For instance, computers will be much smaller and cheaper.
A Cheaper is good.
B Oh, yeah! And he says that computers will be everywhere, like in the furniture, in the walls, in eyeglasses, in our clothes … You'll be able to wear a tiny little computer in your tie.
A But I don't have a tie!
B Well, you could wear it in your scarf! And computers in the future—get this—they will understand your voice! And he says that the Internet will be free, and … Oh, yeah … and most people will have robots in their homes that understand speech, too.

A Will the robots talk?
B Sure. They'll talk, listen, think … everything.
A Sounds weird. Hey, maybe you could get a robot girlfriend.
B Hey! Anyway, scientists will understand everything about our DNA. They'll have a map of all the human genes, about 100,000 of them, and then they'll be able to predict diseases before we get them.
A Is that good?
B Well, if they know you're likely to get a certain disease, they'll be able to fix your genes before you even get sick. And if you get sick, they'll be able to produce medicines just for you because they know your personal DNA.
A Cool! What else is going to happen?
B Well, scientists will grow organs—new livers, kidneys, hearts, and lungs.
A Whoa!
B Yeah, and people will live 'til about 130 or 150.
A 150? Sounds freaky!
B And we'll use new forms of energy, like solar energy, from the sun.
A Don't we already have that?
B Yeah, but it's expensive. If solar energy gets cheaper and easier to use, then everyone will use it, so we'll have less pollution. We'll also have efficient cars that use both electricity and gas at the same time. In fact, someday cars won't use gas at all.
A Great. My car won't run out of gas anymore. What else is going to happen?
B People will travel to other planets. There may even be time travel some day.
A Wow, this is really interesting. Can I borrow that book?

T 9.5 Hot verbs

1. I did some shopping while I was in town. I bought myself a new sweater.
2. "I don't know if I love Tom or Henry." "Make up your mind. You can't marry both of them."
3. Bye-bye! See you soon. Take care of yourself.
4. Aachoo! Oh, no! I think I'm getting a cold.
5. "Are the doors locked?" "I think so, but I'll just make sure."

T 9.6 In a hotel

R = Receptionist   G = Guest

R Thank you for calling the Molokai Grand Hotel. Cathy speaking. How can I help you?
G I'd like to make a reservation.
R For what dates?
G It's for two nights, the thirteenth and the fourteenth of this month.
R And do you want a single or a double room?
G A single. Non-smoking if it's available.
R OK. Yes, that's fine. I have a room for you. And your name is?
G Robert Palmer. Can you tell me what the rate is?
R Yes. That's $150 a night. Would you like to guarantee your reservation with a credit card?
G Yes, sure. It's a Visa. 4929-7983-0621-8849.
R Thank you. And could I have a telephone number please?
G Uh-huh. It's (954) 915-0970.
R You're all set, Mr. Palmer. We look forward to seeing you on the thirteenth. Bye-bye.
G Thanks a lot. Good-bye.

Unit 10

T 10.1 **Don't look down**

I have always enjoyed walking. When I was a boy, I used to go walking on weekends with my father. We went camping and climbing together.

I try to visit a new place every year. Last year I decided to walk a path in Spain called "El camino del rey", which means "the King's Way." It is one of the highest and most dangerous footpaths in Europe. It used to be very safe, but now it's falling down.

I took a train to the village of El Chorro and started to walk toward the mountains. I was very excited.

Then the adventure began. The path was about three feet [one meter] wide, and there were holes in it. It used to have a handrail, but not any more. I didn't know what to do—should I go on my hands and knees, or stand up? I decided to stand up and walk very slowly. At times the path was only as wide as my two boots. I stopped to take a rest, but there was nowhere to sit.

I began to feel very frightened. It was impossible to look down or look up. I was concentrating so hard that my body started aching. There was no thrill of danger, no enjoyment of the view. I thought I was going to die.

I finally managed to get to the end. I was shaking, and I was covered in sweat from heat and fear. I fell to the ground, exhausted.

T 10.2 **I used to …**

1. Nowadays I usually go shopping on Saturday, and on Sunday morning I do yard work or play tennis. When I was a child, I used to play sports on Saturday morning. On Sunday the whole family used to get together for Sunday dinner.
2. I used to watch TV and do my homework in the evening. Now I read, or I go out with friends.
3. We go to a hotel somewhere hot and just do nothing. When I was young, we used to go camping. We went to lots of national parks— Yosemite, Yellowstone, the Grand Canyon …
4. I was very athletic. I used to play everything. Baseball, basketball, tennis, swimming, ice-skating. Now I just play tennis. Oh, and walk the dog!
5. I like documentaries and sports. When I was a kid, I used to like cartoons, action movies, and Westerns, you know, like Clint Eastwood or John Wayne.
6. I liked all the usual things that most kids like: ice cream, pizza, candy, soda. I used to love french fries. Still do. Now I eat everything. Except peppers. Really don't like peppers.

T 10.3 **Infinitives**

1. "I'm hungry. I need something to eat."
   "Have a sandwich!"
2. "My CD player's broken. Can you show me how to fix it?"
   "I'm sorry. I don't have a clue."
3. "Don't talk to me. I have nothing to say to you."
   "Oh, no! What have I done wrong?"
4. "Do I turn left or right? I don't know which way to go."
   "Go straight ahead."

5. "I'm bored. I don't have anything to do."
   "Why don't you read the dictionary?"
6. "Can you get some milk?"
   "Sure. Tell me how much to buy."
   "A liter."
7. "I feel lonely. I need somebody to talk to."
   "Come and talk to me. I'm not doing anything."
8. "I'm going to a formal party, but I don't know what to wear."
   "I think you should wear your black dress."

T 10.4 **Listen and repeat**

frightened	terrified
excited	bored
surprised	exhausted

T 10.5 See p. 77

T 10.6 **It came out of the sky**

I = Interviewer   C = Mr. Cooper

I   Mr. Cooper, you claim to have seen a UFO. Is that right?
C   Yes, that's right. It happened about a year ago.
I   And where was this?
C   It all took place near my home in Nevada.
I   And what time of day was it?
C   It was about one o'clock in the morning. I was having trouble sleeping, so I was awake watching TV.
I   What was the weather like?
C   It was a warm and clear night and there was a full moon.
I   So, Mr. Cooper, what exactly happened?
C   Well, like I said, I was watching TV. Suddenly—all the lights went out. And instead, there was this bright light shining in the windows from the backyard. So I got up and went over to the window to see what it could be.
I   And what did you see?
J   I saw a bright light up in the air, coming toward the house. It was coming closer and closer and getting bigger and bigger. Then it started to land. It landed behind some trees.
I   Did anyone else see it?
C   No. I live alone. So it was just me.
I   What did you do?
C   I went outside to see what it was. Maybe it was an airplane or a helicopter or something—I couldn't tell. Anyway, I saw two forms, you know, two aliens, coming toward me.
I   What did they look like?
C   They were pretty small, about the size of children. They were dressed in green suits, and they were wearing green helmets with red visors so I couldn't see their faces.
I   Did they speak to you?
C   Yes. The one on the right said, "You must come with us."
I   Weren't you scared? I mean, weren't you surprised that they spoke English?
C   They spoke English with a funny accent. It sounded more like a machine talking than a person. At first, I was amazed and very, very scared. But then they touched me and suddenly I wasn't scared anymore. I don't know why. Then they carried me toward the light. But we didn't really walk, we just glided over the ground until we came to the spaceship.
I   And what did their spaceship look like?
C   It was about 45 feet across. It was silver and it

was very, very shiny. And there were round windows all around the sides.
I   Did you go inside?
C   Yes. A door opened and there were steps. So we went in.
I   What did it look like inside?
C   It was all black with lots of colored lights all around. I couldn't see any seats or controls or anything. All there was was a central column going up from the floor to the ceiling, right in the middle of the room.
I   Then what happened?
C   Suddenly, one of the aliens pointed and said, "Stand over there." So I went over and suddenly a bright red light started to shine on me. After a minute or so, the alien said "What is your age?" And I answered, "74." He said, "Turn around." So I did. After a few more minutes, the alien said, "You are too old for our purposes. You may leave now." So the two aliens carried me back outside.
I   Then did the spaceship take off?
C   Yes. I heard a very high-pitched noise, almost like a scream, and the spaceship took off straight up in the air—zoom!—and disappeared!
I   So, what did you do?
C   The next morning I called the police and told them what happened. Then in the afternoon, someone from the government came to my house to interview me. He never told me his name.
I   What did this government agent want to know?
C   He asked me lots of questions about the spaceship and about the aliens. And he said, "Please don't tell anyone about this. It must remain a secret." I thought this was strange, but I didn't say anything to anybody.
I   So, Mr. Cooper, why have you decided to tell everyone about it now?
C   Because I want people to know what happened to me. I think the government is trying to keep UFOs a secret. People have a right to know the truth.
I   Thank you very much, Mr. Cooper, for sharing your story with us.

T 10.7 see p. 81

T 10.8 **Listen and check**

1. Their house is such a mess! I don't know how they can live in it.
2. There were so many people at the party! There was nowhere to dance.
3. I'm so hungry! I could eat a horse.
4. Jane and Pete are such nice people! But I can't stand their kids.
5. I spent so much money this weekend! I don't know where it all went.
6. A present! For me? That's so sweet! You really didn't have to.
7. We had such a good time! Thank you so much for inviting us.
8. Princess is such a smart dog! She understands every word I say.

Unit 11

T 11.1 **Questions and answers**

1. When was the first hamburger made?
   In 1895.
2. When was the first McDonald's opened?
   In 1948.
3. Where were the first hamburgers made?
   In Connecticut.
4. Who were they made by?
   Louis Lassen.
5. Why were they called hamburgers?
   Because the recipe came from Hamburg.
6. How many McDonald's restaurants have been opened since 1948?
   Over 26,000.
7. How many hamburgers are eaten every day?
   35 million.

T 11.2 **Listen and check**

1. A Are Coca-Cola and hamburgers sold *only* in the United States?
   B No, they aren't. They're sold all over the world.
2. A Was Coca-Cola invented by Louis Lassen?
   B No, it wasn't. It was invented by John Pemberton.
3. A Were the first hamburgers made in 1948?
   B No, they weren't. They were made in 1895.
4. A Was the first McDonald's restaurant opened in New York City?
   B No, it wasn't. It was opened in San Bernardino, California.
5. A Have 2,600 restaurants now been opened worldwide?
   B No, not 2,600. Over 26,000 have been opened worldwide.

T 11.3 **The history of chewing gum**

P = Presenter   I = Interviewer
LW = Leanne Ward, chewing gum expert
A & B = Interviewees

Part One

P Today on *Worldly Wise,* the world's most common habit … .
   Yes, chewing gum. We chew 100,000 tons of it every year but how many of us actually know what it's made of?
I Excuse me, I see you're chewing gum …
A Yeah.
I Do you have any idea what it's made of?
A Nah—no idea. Never thought about it.
I Do *you* have any idea what chewing gum is made of?
B … Uhh, no, not a clue. Rubber maybe?
I And do you have any idea who invented it?
A I don't know!
B Me either!
I An American?
B Yeah—sure—I guess it was invented by an American, yeah.
P Well, it wasn't! Believe it or not, it wasn't an American who invented chewing gum. It was invented in Sweden. In Sweden?! I hear you say. But listen to Leanne Ward, a chewing gum expert.
LW The history of chewing goes back thousands of years. In Sweden in 1993, the skeleton of a teenager was found—he was 9,000 years old. And in his mouth was a gum made of tree sap and sweetened with honey—the first known chewing gum.

P It seems we've always chewed things with no real food value. Babies are born wanting to chew. Everything goes straight into their mouths. So why do we chew? Here's Leanne again.
LW We chew to clean our teeth and freshen our breath but also because we just like chewing. The ancient Greeks chewed a gum called *mastica,* which is a type of tree sap. They thought it was good for their health and women really enjoyed chewing it as a way to sweeten their breath. Then in the first century AD we know that the Mayan Indians in Central America liked to chew a tree sap, called *chiclay.* They wrapped it in leaves and put it in their mouths so this was, if you like, the first pack of chewing gum. The American Indians also chewed tree sap—they gave it to the English settlers when they arrived, but it wasn't until a few hundred years later, that it became really popular in America.

T 11.4 **Part Two**

P The history of modern chewing gum begins in nineteenth century America. In 1892 a bright young salesman named William Wrigley decided that chewing gum was the thing of the future. Wrigley was a business genius. He was the first to use advertising to sell in a big way. Here's Leanne.
LW William Wrigley was really an advertising genius. He hired hundreds of pretty girls, who he called "the Wrigley girls." They walked up and down the streets of Chicago and New York City handing out free gum. Millions of pieces were given away. He also had huge electric signs and billboards—one billboard was a mile long—it ran along the side of the train track. So with all this, chewing gum became very popular all over the US.
P So how did the world get to know and love chewing gum? Leanne again.
LW Well, during the Second World War, American soldiers were given Wrigley's gum to help them relax. In 1944 *all* gum production went to the US Army, and they took their gum overseas and gave it to children. Soon they were followed everywhere by the cry, "Got any gum, chum?"
P And so the popularity of gum spread to other countries. After the war, sales of gum exploded worldwide. Chewing gum was even taken into space by the first astronauts. So what exactly *is* it made of?
LW Well, the strangest thing about gum today is that nobody knows what it's made of. *Nobody* will tell you. The chewing gum industry keeps the recipe top secret.

T 11.5 **Everyday conversations**

1. Dad, are we there yet?
   No. We won't be there for another two hours, but we'll stop soon and get something to eat.
   OK. I need to go to the bathroom, too.
2. Good evening. Table for two?
   Yes, please.
   Smoking or non-smoking?
   Non-smoking.
   This way, please.
3. Hi. I need $10 worth of gas.
   Which pump?

Uhh … pump number … five.
That's $10 … out of 20. And here's your change. Have a nice day.
4. Good evening, ladies and gentlemen and welcome to Eastern Airlines' Flight 62 nonstop service to Atlanta. We'd like to begin boarding our first class passengers, passengers with small children, and any passengers requiring special assistance. Please have your boarding passes ready for inspection.
5. Excuse me!!
   Oh, sorry!

Unit 12

T 12.1 **Sweet dreams**

If I were a princess, I'd live in a palace. I'd have servants to take care of me. My Mom would be queen, and she wouldn't work. I wouldn't go to school. I'd have a private teacher. I'd ride a white horse, and I'd wear a long dress. I could have all the ice cream I wanted.

T 12.2 **see p. 92**

T 12.3 *If I were you …*

1. I don't have any money. What am I going to do?
   If I were you, I'd try to spend less.
   What do you mean?
   Well, you buy a lot of clothes, designer clothes. Stop buying such expensive clothes.
   But I like them!
2. My hair looks awful. I can't do anything with it.
   It's not that bad.
   Oh, yes it is. Just look at it.
   Well, if I were you, I'd try that new hairstylist, Antonio. He's supposed to be very good, and not that expensive.
   Mmm. OK, I'll try him. Thanks.
3. I have a toothache.
   Have you seen a dentist?
   No.
   Well, if I were you, I'd make an appointment right away.
4. I had a fight with my boyfriend.
   About what?
   Oh, the usual thing. He gets jealous if I just look at another guy.
   And did you?
   No, of course not!
   Well, if I were you, I'd forget about him. He won't ever change, you know.
   Oh, I couldn't do that.
5. My car won't start in the morning.
   If I were you, I'd buy a new one. Yours is so old.
   I know it's old, but I can't afford a new one.
   Then take it to a mechanic and get it fixed.
   All right.
6. My neighbors make a lot of noise.
   Do they? That's awful.
   Yeah. We can't get to sleep at night.
   Have you spoken to them about it?
   No, we're too frightened.
   If I were you, I'd invite them over for coffee and say that you're having problems.
   That's probably a good idea. I'm not sure they'd come, but I'll try it.

Ruth

I'm going to take a vacation in Mexico for a couple of weeks and stay in a beachfront hotel in Acapulco. Then I'm going to look for a job. I want to work in media—advertising or journalism would be perfect.

My sister and I are going to rent an apartment together, so we'll have to start looking soon. I'm very excited about the future. And I'm also very ambitious!

Henry

I'm not sure yet. Some friends have invited me to go to San Francisco with them, so I might go to California. I'll have to earn some money, so I might work in a restaurant for a while.

I don't know what I want to do. I love France, so I might live in Paris for a while. I could make some money painting portraits in Montmartre. Who knows? I might meet a beautiful French woman and fall in love! Wouldn't that be wonderful!

T 12.5 **Ghost stories**

I = Interviewer   A = Alice Lester
I When did you first hear these voices, Alice?
A Well, I was at home, sitting down, and reading.
I And what did they say?
A The first time, there was just one voice. It said, "Don't be afraid, I just want to help you."
I But it didn't say how it wanted to help you?
A No, it didn't. It just went away.
I And what about the second time?
A It was while I was away on a trip, but this time there were two voices. They told me to go back home immediately because there was something wrong with me.
I So is that what you did?
A Yes. And when I was back home, the voices gave me an address to go to.
I And what was the address?
A Well, now it starts to get very strange. The address was the brain scan department of a hospital. I went there and I met Dr. Abrams, who is a consultant. As I was meeting him, the voices said to me, "Tell him you have a tumor in your brain, and that you're in a lot of danger." I said this to Dr. Abrams, but I know he didn't believe me. Anyway, they gave me a brain scan, and I did have a tumor!
I What an incredible story! Did you have an operation?
A Yes, I did. And after the operation, the voices came back again, and they said "We're happy we were able to help you. Good-bye." And I've been in good health ever since. Now, what do you think of that?

T 12.6 **Everyday conversations**

1. A Excuse me! Can I get past?
   B Pardon me?
   A Can I get past, please?
   B Oh, I'm sorry. I didn't hear you. Yes, of course.
   A Thanks a lot.
2. A I hear you're going to get married soon. Congratulations!
   B That's right, next July. July 21. Can you come to the wedding?
   A July 21? Oh, what a shame! That's when I'm away on vacation.
   C Don't worry. We'll send you some pictures.

A That's very nice of you.
3. A Uh-oh! Look at the time! Hurry up, or we'll miss the train.
   B Just a minute! I can't find my umbrella. Do you know where it is?
   A I have no idea. But you won't need it. It's a beautiful day. Just look at the sky!
   B Oh, all right. I'm ready. Let's go.
4. A Good luck on your exam!
   B Same to you. I hope we both pass.
   A Did you go out last night?
   B No, of course not. I went to bed early. What about you?
   A Me, too. See you later. After the exam, let's go out for coffee.
   B Good idea.

Unit 13

T 13.1 **Andy's story**

1. How long have you been sleeping on the streets?
   For a year. It was very cold at first, but you get used to it.
2. Why did you come to New York?
   I came here to look for work, and I never left.
3. How long have you been selling *Street News*?
   For six months. I'm outside the subway station seven days a week selling the paper.
4. Have you made many friends?
   Lots. But I can't stand it when people think I drink or take drugs. My problem is I'm homeless. I want a job, but I need somewhere to live before I can get a job. So I need money to get somewhere to live, but I can't get money because I can't get a job, and I can't get a job because I don't have a place to live. So I'm trapped.
5. How many copies do you sell a day?
   Usually about 50.
6. How many copies have you sold today?
   So far, ten. But it's still early.

T 13.2 **Make questions**

1. How long have you been trying to find a job?
2. How many jobs have you had?
3. How long have you been standing here today?
4. How did you lose your job?
5. How long have you had your dog?
6. Who's your best friend?
7. Where did you meet him?
8. How long have you known each other?

T 13.3

1. How long have you been trying to find a job?
   For over a year. It's been really hard.
2. How many jobs have you had?
   About 20, maybe more. I've done everything.
3. How long have you been standing here today?
   Since 8:00 this morning, and I'm freezing.
4. How did you lose your job?
   I had a small company, but it went out of business, and then I started having health problems, but without the job, I didn't have health insurance anymore, so things got worse.
5. How long have you had your dog?
   I've had him for about two months, that's all.
6. Who's your best friend?
   A guy named Bob, who's also from Pennsylvania, like me.
7. Where did you meet him?

I met him here in New York.
8. How long have you known each other?
   Almost a year. I met him right after I came to New York.

T 13.4 see T 13.5

T 13.5 **Phoning home**

C = Craig   M = His mother
C Hi, Mom. It's me, Craig.
M Craig! Hello! How nice to hear from you. How are you? How's the new job going?
C Work's OK … I think . I'm just … so …
M Tired? You sound tired. Are you tired? What have you been doing?
C I *am* tired, really tired. I've been working so hard and everything's so new to me. I'm in the office until eight o'clock every night.
M Eight o'clock! Every night? That's terrible. And when do you eat? Have you been eating well?
C Yes, yes—I've been eating OK. After work, Linda and I go out for something to eat in the coffee shop around the corner. We're too tired to cook.
M Linda? Who's Linda?
C Linda? Oh, Linda. I'm sure I've told you about her. We work together in the same office— she's been working here for a while, so she's been helping me a lot. She's really nice. You'd like her Mom, if you met her. She lives near me.
M Mmm. Maybe you told your father about her, but not me. I've certainly never heard you talk about Linda before.
C Ah, yes. Dad. How is he? What's he been doing lately?
M Well, he's just returned from a business trip to Canada, so he didn't go to work today … he's been relaxing.
C Oh, yeah. He's been working in Ottawa, hasn't he? Well, I'm glad he's relaxing now. And what about you, Mom?
M Well, I was going to call you actually. I'm coming to San Francisco next Tuesday. I'm going to a teachers' conference there, and I wondered if I could stay at your apartment.
C Next Tuesday. That's great! Of course you can stay here. I'll try to leave work early that day and I'll meet you after the conference. You can meet Linda, too. We'll go out for dinner.
M Wonderful! I'm looking forward to it already.
C Me, too. See you next week. Give my love to Dad!
M Bye, Honey. Take care.
C Bye, Mom.

T 13.6 see p. 105

T 13.7 **Phone numbers**

061 501277
633488
01923 272944
0797 0800 994
020 7927 4863

P = Peter   J = John

1. **P** Hello?
   J Hello, Peter. This is John.
   P Hi, John. How are you?
   J Fine, thanks. How about you?
   P All right. Did you have a nice weekend? You went away, didn't you?
   J Yes, we went to see some friends who live in the country. It was great. We had a good time.
   P Oh, good.
   J Peter, could you do me a favor? I'm playing squash tonight, but my racquet's broken. Could I borrow yours?
   P Sure, no problem.
   J Thanks a lot. I'll come and get it in half an hour, if that's OK.
   P Yeah, I'll be here.
   J OK. Bye.
   P Bye.

A = Receptionist   B = student
C = Ann, teacher

2. **A** Good morning. International School of English.
   B Hello, could I speak to Ann Baker, please?
   A One moment, please.
   C Hello?
   A Hello. Can I speak to Ann Baker, please?
   C Speaking.
   A Oh, hello. I saw your advertisement about English classes in a magazine. Could you send me some information, please?
   C Of course. Can I have your name and address, please?

A = Mike's roommate   B = Jim

3. **A** Hello.
   B Hello. Mike?
   A I'm sorry, but Mike's out right now. Who's calling?
   B Jim, his friend from work.
   A Can I take a message?
   B Yeah. Can you tell him that I called, and I'll try again later. Do you know what time he'll be back?
   A In about an hour, I think.
   B OK, thanks. Good-bye.
   A Bye.

Unit 14

T 14.1 see p. 106

T 14.2 **Listen and check**

I was delighted because I'd passed all my exams.
I was hungry because I hadn't had any breakfast.
I went to bed early because I'd had a busy day.
Our teacher was angry because we hadn't done the homework.
My leg was sore because I had hurt it playing soccer.
The plants died because I'd forgotten to water them.
The house was a mess because we'd had a party the night before.

T 14.3 **Which sentences contain *had*?**

1. When we arrived she left.
2. When we arrived she'd left.
3. She'd like to leave now.
4. We'd stopped playing when the rain started.

5. We stopped playing when the rain started.
6. We'd play tennis if the rain stopped.
7. He checked that he'd turned off his cell phone.
8. He turned off the television and went to bed.
9. I couldn't believe that I'd lost my passport again.
10. If I lost my passport, I'd be very upset.

T 14.4 **What does Mary say?**

I love John very much.
We met six months ago.
I've never been in love before.
We're very happy.
I'll love him forever.
I'm seeing him this evening.

T 14.5 **What did Mary tell you?**

Mary told me that she loved John very much. She said that they'd met six months ago and that she'd never been in love before. She told me that they were very happy and that she'd love him forever. She said that she was seeing him that evening.

T 14.6 **An interview with Carmen Day**

I = Interviewer   CD = Carmen Day

I Carmen, why have you written another romantic novel?
CD Because I find romantic fiction easy to write, but my next novel won't be a romance. I'm hoping to write something different, maybe a detective story.
I In *One Short Hot Summer,* who is the character of Brad based on?
CD Ah, well he's based on my first husband, Charles Ford, the actor. Charles made me very unhappy, you know.
I You say your "first" husband—Have you remarried?
CD Oh, yes. I've been married for nearly ten years to Tony—Tony Marsh.
I Is he an actor, too?
CD No, he's a lawyer.
I And are you happy now?
CD Very. I can honestly say that I've found happiness again. Tony and I are extremely happy together.
I Carmen, how many novels have you written so far?
CD Well, I've now written five novels, and three stories for children.
I And when do you think you'll stop writing?
CD Never. I'll never stop. I'll continue to write even when I'm an old lady.

T 14.7

In an interview, Carmen said she had written another romantic novel because she found romantic fiction easy to write, but that her next novel would be something different, possibly a detective story.

Carmen said that the character of Brad was based on her first husband, Charles Ford, the actor, who had made her very unhappy. But she added that she was now married to Tony Marsh, who is a lawyer. She said that they had been married for nearly ten years and that they were extremely happy together.

She told me that she had now written five novels, and also that she had written three stories for children. She said she would never stop writing, not even when she was an old lady.

T 14.8 **"Talk to me"**

Well every night I see a light up in your window
But every night you won't answer the door
But although you won't ever let me in
From the street I can see your silhouette sitting close to him
What must I do?
What does it take
To get you to
Talk to me
Until the night is over
Talk to me
Well until the night is over, yeah yeah yeah
I got a full week's pay
And baby I've been working hard all day
I'm not asking for the world, you see
I'm just asking girl
Talk to me
Well late at night I hear music that you're playing soft and low
Yes and late at night I see the two of you swaying so close
I don't understand darling what was my sin?
Why am I down here below while you're up there with him?
What did I do?
What did I say?
What must I pay
To get you to
Talk to me
Until the night is over
Talk to me
Well until the night is over, yeah yeah yeah
I got a full week's pay
And baby I've been working hard all day
I'm not asking for the world you see
I'm just asking girl
Talk to me.

T 14.9 **Saying good-bye**

a. Good-bye! Drive carefully and call us when you get there!
b. Bye! Have a nice weekend.
c. Good-bye! Have a safe trip. Send us a postcard!
d. Good-bye. Here's my number. Just call me if you have any problems with it.
e. Good-bye. It's been very interesting talking to you. We'll let you know in the next week or so.
f. Good-bye! Good luck in the future. I've really enjoyed our classes together!
g. Bye-bye! Thank you for inviting me to the party.
h. Good-bye. Thank you for a wonderful evening. You'll have to come over to our place next time.

Grammar Reference

Unit 1

1.1 Tenses

This unit has examples of the Present Simple and Present Continuous, the Past Simple, and two future forms: *going to* and the Present Continuous for the future.
All these tenses are covered again in later units.
Present tenses   Unit 2
Past tenses   Unit 3
Future forms   Units 5 and 9
The aim in this unit is to review what you know.

Present tenses
> He **lives** with his parents.
> She **speaks** three languages.
> I**'m enjoying** the class.
> They**'re studying** at a university.

Past tense
> He **went** to England last year.
> She **came** to the United States three years ago.

Future forms
> I**'m going to work** as an interpreter.
> What **are** you **doing** tonight?

1.2 Questions

Questions with question words
1. Questions can begin with a question word.

what	where	which	how
who	when	why	whose

> **Where**'s the station?
> **Why** are you laughing?
> **Whose** is this coat?
> **How** does she go to work?

2. *What*, *which*, and *whose* can be followed by a noun.
> **What size** do you take?
> **What kind** of music do you like?
> **Which coat** is yours?
> **Whose book** is this?

3. *Which* is generally used when there is a limited choice.
> **Which** is your coat? The black one or the red one?
> This rule is not always true.
> **What**
> **Which** | newspaper do you read?

4. *How* can be followed by an adjective or an adverb.
> **How big** is his new car?
> **How fast** does it go?
> *How* can also be followed by *much* or *many*.
> **How much** is this sandwich?
> **How many** brothers and sisters do you have?

Questions with no question word
The answer to these questions is *Yes* or *No*.
> Are you hot?   Yes, I am./No, I'm not.
> Is she working?   Yes, she is./No, she isn't.
> Does he smoke?   Yes, he does./No, he doesn't.
> Can you swim?   Yes, I can./No, I can't.

Form

Verb forms with an auxiliary verb

Affirmative	Question
She is reading.	Is she reading?
They are watching a movie.	What are they watching?
She can drive.	Can she drive?

Verb forms with no auxiliary verb
In the Present Simple and the Past Simple there is no auxiliary verb in the affirmative.
> They **live** in Honolulu.
> He **arrived** yesterday.
Do/does/did is used in the question.
> **Do** they **live** in Honolulu?
> Where **does** Bill **come** from?
> When **did** he **arrive?**

Unit 2

2.1 Present Simple

Form

Affirmative and negative

I We You They	live don't live	
He She It	lives doesn't live	near here.

Question

Where	do	I we you they	live?
	does	he she it	

Short answer

Do you like Peter? Does she speak Thai?	Yes, I do. No, she doesn't.

Use

The Present Simple is used to express:
1. a habit.
     I **get up** at 7:30.
     Cindy **smokes** too much.
2. a fact that is always true.
     Vegetarians **don't eat** meat.
     We **come** from Brazil.
3. a fact that is true for a long time.
     I **live** in Miami.
     She **works** in a bank.

2.2 Present Continuous

Form

am/is/are + *-ing* (present participle)

Affirmative and negative

I	'm (am) 'm not	
He She It	's (is) isn't	working.
We You They	're (are) aren't	

Question

What	am	I	wearing?
	is	he she it	
	are	we you they	

Short answer

Are you going? Is Ana working?	Yes, I am./No, I'm not. Yes, she is./No, she isn't.	NOT Yes, ~~I'm.~~ Yes, ~~she's.~~

Use

The Present Continuous is used to express:
1. an activity happening now.
     They**'re playing** soccer in the backyard.
     She can't answer the phone because she**'s washing** her hair.
2. an activity happening around now, but perhaps not at the moment of speaking.
     She**'s studying** math at the university.
     I**'m reading** a good book by Henry James.
3. a planned future arrangement.
     I**'m meeting** Ms. Boyd at ten o'clock tomorrow.
     What **are** you **doing** this evening?

2.3 Present Simple and Present Continuous

1. Look at the wrong sentences, and compare them with the correct sentences.

✗	Hank is coming from Canada.
✓	Hank comes from Canada.
✗	This is a great party. Everyone has a good time.
✓	This is a great party. Everyone is having a good time.
✗	I read a good book right now.
✓	I'm reading a good book right now.

2. There are some verbs that are usually used in the Present Simple only. They express a state, not an activity.

✓	I like soda.
✗	I'm liking soda.

   Other verbs like this are *think, agree, understand, love.*

2.4 have/have got

Form

Affirmative

I We You They	have	two sisters.
He She	has	

Negative

I We You They	don't have	any money.
He She	doesn't have	

Question

Do	I we you they	have a car?
Does	he she	

Short answer

Do you have a camera?	Yes, I do./No, I don't.

We can use contractions (*'ve* and *'s*) with *have got*, but not with *have*.
> **I've got** a sister
> I **have** a sister.   NOT ~~I've a sister.~~

Use

1. *Have* and *have got* mean the same. *Have got* is informal. We use it a lot when we speak, but not when we write.
    > **Have** you **got** a dog?
    > The prime minister **has** a meeting with the president today.
    In American English, *have + do/does* is much more common.
2. When *have* + noun expresses an activity or a habit, *have* and the *do/does/don't/doesn't* forms are used. *Have got* is not used. Compare these sentences.

✗	I've got breakfast in the morning.
✓	I have breakfast in the morning.

✗	What time have you got lunch?
✓	What time do you have lunch?

✗	He has never got milk in his coffee.
✓	He never has milk in his coffee.

4 In the past tense, the *got* forms are unusual. *Had* with *did* and *didn't* is much more common.
    > I **had** a bicycle when I was young.
    > My parents **had** a lot of books in the house.
    > **Did** you **have** a nice weekend?
    > I **didn't have** any money when I was a student.

Unit 3

3.1 Past Simple

Spelling

1. The normal rule is to add *-ed*.
    > work**ed**   start**ed**
    If the verb ends in *-e*, add *-d*.
    > live**d**   love**d**
2. If the verb has only one syllable + one vowel + one consonant, double the consonant.
    > sto**pp**ed   pla**nn**ed
3. If the verb ends in a consonant + *-y*, change the *-y* to *-ied*.
    > stud**ied**   carr**ied**
    There are many common irregular verbs. See the list on p. 153.

Form

The form of the Past Simple is the same for all persons.

Affirmative

I He/She/It We You They	finished arrived went	yesterday.

Negative

The negative of the Past Simple is formed with *didn't*.
> He walk̶ed̶.
> He **didn't** walk ☐.

I He/She/It We You They	didn't (did not)	arrive yesterday.

Question

The question in the Past Simple is formed with *did*.
> She finish̶ed̶.
> When **did** she finish ☐?

When did	she you they etc.	arrive?

Short answer

Did you go to work yesterday? Did it rain last night?	Yes, I did. No, it didn't.

Use

1. The Past Simple expresses a past action that is now finished.
    > We **played** tennis last Sunday.
    > I **worked** in Tokyo from 1994 to 1999.
    > John **left** two minutes ago.
2. Notice the time expressions that are used with the Past Simple.

I did it	last year. last month. five years ago. yesterday morning. in 1985.

3.2 Past Continuous

Form

was/were + -ing
(present participle)

Affirmative and negative

I He She It	was wasn't (was not)	
We You They	were weren't (were not)	working.

Question

	was	I he she it	
What			doing?
	were	we you they	

Short answer

Were you working yesterday?	Yes, I was.
Was she studying when you arrived?	No, she wasn't.

Use

1. The Past Continuous expresses a past activity that has duration.
    > I met her while I **was living** in Kyoto.
    > You **were making** a lot of noise last night.
    > What **were** you **doing**?
2. The activity began *before* the action expressed by the Past Simple.
    > She **was making** coffee when we arrived.
    > When I phoned Paulo he **was having** dinner.
3. The Past Continuous expresses an activity in progress before, and probably after, a time in the past.
    > When I woke up this morning, the sun **was shining**.
    > What **were** you **doing** at 8:00 last night?

3.3 Past Simple and Past Continuous

1. The Past Simple expresses past actions as simple facts.
    > I **did** my homework last night.
    > "What **did** you **do** yesterday evening?" "I **watched** TV."
2. The Past Continuous gives past activities time and duration. The activity can be interrupted.
    > "What **were** you **doing** at 8:00?" "I **was watching** TV."
    > I **was doing** my homework when Jane arrived.
3. In stories, the Past Continuous can describe the scene. The Past Simple tells the action.
    > It **was** a beautiful day. The sun **was shining** and the birds **were singing**, so we **decided** to go for a picnic. We **put** everything in the car …
4. The questions below refer to different time periods. The Past Continuous asks about activities before, and the Past Simple asks about what happened after.

What were you doing What did you do	when it started to rain?	We were playing tennis. We went home.

3.4 Prepositions in time expressions

at	in	no preposition
at six o'clock at midnight at Christmas	in the morning/afternoon/evening in December in the summer in 1995 in two weeks' time	today yesterday tomorrow the day after tomorrow the day before yesterday last night last week two weeks ago next month yesterday evening tomorrow evening this evening tonight
on		
on Saturday on Monday morning on Christmas day on January 18 on the weekend		

Unit 4

4.1 Expressions of quantity

Count and noncount nouns

1. It is important to understand the difference between count and noncount nouns.

Count nouns	Noncount nouns
a cup	water
a girl	sugar
an apple	milk
an egg	music
a kilo	money

We can say *three cups, two girls, ten kilos*. We can count them. We cannot say ~~two waters~~, ~~three musics~~, ~~one money~~. We cannot count them.

2. Count nouns can be singular or plural.
> This **cup is** full.
> These **cups are** empty.

Noncount nouns can only be singular.
> The **water is** cold.
> The **weather was** terrible.

much and *many*

1. We use *much* with noncount nouns in questions and negatives.
> How **much money** do you have?
> There isn't **much milk** left.
2. We use *many* with count nouns in questions and negatives.
> How **many people** were at the party?
> I didn't take **many photos** on vacation.

some and *any*

1. *Some* is used in affirmative sentences.
> I'd like **some** sugar.
2. *Any* is used in questions and negatives.
> Is there **any** sugar in this coffee?
> Do you have **any** brothers and sisters?
> We don't have **any** dishwashing liquid.
> I didn't buy **any** apples.
3. We use *some* in questions that are requests or offers.
> Can I have **some** cake?
> Would you like **some** soda?
4. The rules are the same for the compounds *someone, anything, anybody, somewhere*, etc.
> I have **something** for you.
> Hello? Is **anybody** here?
> There isn't **anywhere** to go in my town.

a few and *a little*

1. We use *a few* with count nouns.
> There are **a few eggs** left, but not many.
2. We use *a little* with noncount nouns.
> Can you give me **a little help**?

a lot/lots of

1. We use *a lot/lots of* with both count and noncount nouns.
> There's **a lot of butter**.
> I have **lots of friends**.
2. *A lot/lots of* can be used in questions and negatives.
> Are there **lots of tourists** in your country?
> There isn't **a lot of butter**, but there's enough.

4.2 Articles—*a* and *the*

1. The indefinite article *a* or *an* is used with singular, countable nouns to refer to a thing or an idea for the first time.
> We have **a cat** and **a dog**.
> There's **a supermarket** on Adam Street.
2. The definite article *the* is used with singular and plural, countable and noncountable nouns when both the speaker and the listener know the thing or idea already.
> We have a cat and a dog. **The cat** is old, but **the dog** is just a puppy.
> I'm going to **the supermarket**. Do you want anything? (We both know which supermarket.)

Indefinite article

The indefinite article is used:
1. with professions.
> I'm **a teacher**.
> She's **an architect**.
2. with some expressions of quantity.
> **a pair of   a little   a couple of   a few**
3. in exclamations with *what* + a count noun.
> **What a** beautiful **day**!
> **What a pity**!

Definite article

The definite article is used:
1. before oceans, rivers, hotels, theaters, museums, and newspapers.
> **the Atlantic   the Metropolitan Museum**
> *The Washington Times*   **the Ritz**
2. if there is only one of something.
> **the sun   the president   the government**
3. with superlative adjectives.
> He's **the richest man** in the world.
> Jane's **the oldest** in the class.

No article

There is no article:
1. before plural and noncountable nouns when talking about things in general.
> I like potatoes.
> Milk is good for you.
2. before countries, towns, streets, languages, magazines, meals, airports, stations, and mountains.
> I had lunch with John.
> I bought *Cosmopolitan* at South Station.
3. before some places and with some forms of transportation.

> at home   in/to bed   at/to work   at/to school
> by bus   by plane   by car   by train   on foot

> She goes to work by bus.
> I was at home yesterday evening.
4. in exclamations with *what* + a noncount noun.
> **What** beautiful **weather**!
> **What** loud **music**!

Note

In the phrase *go home*, there is no article and no preposition.
> I **went home** early.   NOT   ~~I went to home~~.

Unit 5

5.1 Verb patterns 1

Here are four verb patterns. There is a list of verb patterns on p. 153.
1. Verb + to + infinitive
   They **want to buy a** new car.
   I'd **like to go** abroad.
2. Verb + -ing
   Everyone **loves going** to parties.
   He **finished reading** his book.
3. Verb + -ing or + to + infinitive with no change in meaning
   It **began to rain/raining**.
   I **continued to work/working** in the library.
4. Verb + preposition + -ing
   We**'re thinking of moving**.
   I**'m looking forward to having** more free time.

5.2 *like doing* and *would like to do*

1. *Like doing* and *love doing* express a general enjoyment.
   I **like working** as a teacher. = I am a teacher and I enjoy it.
   I **love dancing**. = This is one of my hobbies.
2. *Would like to do* and *would love to do* express a preference now or at a specific time.
   I**'d like to be** a teacher. = When I grow up, I want to be a teacher.
   Thank you. I**'d love to dance**. = We're at a club. I'm pleased that you asked me.

Question	Short answer
Would you like to dance?	Yes, I would./Yes, I'd love to.
Would you like to come for a walk?	Yes, I would./No, thank you.

Note
No, I wouldn't is not common because it is impolite.

5.3 *will*

Form

will + infinitive without *to*
Will is a modal auxiliary verb. There is an introduction to modal auxiliary verbs on p. 147 of the Grammar Reference. The forms of *will* are the same for all persons.

Affirmative and negative

I He/She/It We/You/They	'll (will) won't	come. help you. invite Tom.

Question

When will	he you they	help me?

Short answer

Will you help me?	Yes, I will.

Note
No, I won't is not common because it is impolite. It means "I don't want to help you."
A polite way of saying "no" here is "I'm afraid I can't."

Use

Will is used:
1. to express a future decision or intention made *at* the moment of speaking.
   "It's Jane's birthday." "It is? I**'ll buy** her some flowers."
   I**'ll give** you my phone number.
   "Which do you want? The blue or the red?"
   "I**'ll take** the red, thank you."
2. to express an offer.
   I**'ll carry** your suitcase.
   We**'ll wash** the dishes.

Other uses of *will* are covered in Unit 9.

going to

Form

am/is/are + *going* + *to* + infinitive

Affirmative and negative

I	'm (am) 'm not	
He She It	's (is) isn't	going to work.
We You They	're (are) aren't	

Question

	am	I	
When	is	he she it	going to arrive?
	are	we you they	

Short answer

Are they going to get married?	Yes, they are./No, they aren't.

Use

Going to is used:
1. to express a future decision, intention, or plan made *before* the moment of speaking.
   How long **are** they **going to stay** in Acapulco?
   She **isn't going to have** a birthday party.

   ### Note
   The Present Continuous can be used in a similar way for a plan or arrangement, particularly with the verbs *go* and *come*.
   She**'s coming** on Friday.
   I**'m going** home early tonight.
2. when we can see or feel now that something is certain to happen in the future.
   Look at those clouds! It**'s going to rain**.
   Watch out! That box **is going to fall**.

will or *going to*?
Look at the use of *will* and *going to* in these sentences.
   I'm **going to make** a chicken casserole for dinner.
   (I decided this morning and bought everything for it.)
   What should I cook for dinner? Umm ... I know! I**'ll make** chicken casserole! That's a good idea!
   (I decided at the moment of speaking.)

Unit 6

6.1 What ... like?

Form

what + to be + subject + like?

What	's (is) your teacher are his parents was your holiday were the beaches	like?	She's very patient. They're very kind. Wonderful. We swam a lot. OK, but some were dirty.

Note

We don't use *like* in the answer.
    She's patient.   NOT ~~She's like patient~~.

Use

What ... like? means "Describe somebody or something. Tell me about them. I don't know anything about them."
Like in this question is a preposition, not a verb:
    "What's Jim **like**?" "He's intelligent and kind, and he's got beautiful brown eyes."
In the following sentences *like* is a verb:
    "What does Jim **like**?" "He **likes** motorcycles and playing tennis."

Note

How's your mother? asks about health. It doesn't ask for a description.
    "How's your mother?" "She's very well, thank you."

6.2 Comparative and superlative adjectives

Form

1. Look at the chart.

		Comparative	Superlative
Short adjectives	cheap small *big	cheaper smaller bigger	cheapest smallest biggest
Adjectives that end in -*y*	funny early heavy	funnier earlier heavier	funniest earliest heaviest
Adjectives with two syllables or more	careful boring expensive interesting	more careful more buying more expensive more interesting	most careful most boring most expensive most interesting
Irregular adjectives	far good bad	farther better worse	farthest best worst

   * Short adjectives with one vowel + one consonant double the consonant: *hot/hotter/hottest, fat/fatter/fattest.*

2. *Than* is often used after a comparative adjective.
    I'm **younger than** Barbara.
    Barbara's **more intelligent than** Sara.
  Much can come before the comparative to give emphasis.
    She's **much nicer than** her sister.
    Is Tokyo **much more modern than** New York?

3. *The* is used before superlative adjectives.
    He's **the funniest** student in the class.
    What is **the tallest** building in the world?

Use

1. We use comparatives to compare one thing, person, or action with another.
    She's **taller** than me.
    Tokyo's **more expensive** than Taipei.
2. We use superlatives to compare somebody or something with the whole group.
    She's the **tallest** in the class.
    It's the **most expensive** hotel in the world.
3. *As ... as* shows that something is the same or equal.
    Jim's **as tall as** Peter.
    I'm **as worried as** you are.
4. *Not as/so ... as* shows that something isn't the same or equal.
    She **isn't as tall as** her mother.
    My car **wasn't so expensive as** yours.

Unit 7

7.1 Present Perfect

Form

have/has + -ed (past participle)
The past participle of regular verbs ends in *-ed*. There are many common irregular verbs. See the list on p. 143.

Affirmative and negative

I We/You/They	've (have) haven't	worked in a factory.
He/She/It	's (has) hasn't	

Question

Have	I we/you/they	been to the United States?
Has	he/she/it	

Short answer

Have you been to Korea?	Yes, I have./No, I haven't.
Has she ever written poetry?	Yes, she has./No, she hasn't.

Note

We cannot use *I've, they've, he's*, etc., in short answers.
Yes, I **have**.   NOT ~~Yes, I've.~~
Yes, we **have**.   NOT ~~Yes, we've.~~

Use

1. The Present Perfect looks back from the present into the past, and expresses what has happened before now. The action happened at an indefinite time in the past.
   I've met a lot of famous people. (before now)
   She **has won** awards. (in her life)
   She**'s written** 20 songs. (up to now)
   The action can continue to the present, and probably into the future.
   She**'s lived** here for 20 years. (she still lives here)

2. The Present Perfect expresses an experience as part of someone's life.
   I've traveled a lot in Asia.
   They**'ve lived** all over the world.
   Ever and *never* are common with this use.
   Have you **ever** been in a car crash?
   My mother has **never** flown in a plane.

3. The Present Perfect expresses an action or state which began in the past and continues to the present.
   I've known Alicia for six years.
   How long **have** you **worked** as a teacher?
   Note that the time expressions *for* and *since* are common with this use. We use *for* with a period of time, and *since* with a point in time.
   We've lived here **for** two years. (a period of time)
   I've had a beard **since** I left the army. (a point in time)

Note

In many languages, this use is expressed by a present tense. But in English, we say:
   Peter **has been** a teacher for ten years.
   NOT   ~~Peter is a teacher for ten years.~~

4. The Present Perfect expresses a past action with results in the present. It is often a recent past action.
   I've lost my wallet. (I don't have it now.)
   The taxi**'s arrived**. (It's outside the door now.)
   Has the mail carrier **been**? (Are there any letters for me?)
   The adverbs *just, already*, and *yet* are common with this use. *Yet* is used in questions and negatives.
   She's **just** had some good news.
   I've **already** had breakfast.
   Has the mail carrier been **yet**?
   It's 11:00 and she hasn't gotten up **yet**.

7.2 Present Perfect and Past Simple

1. Compare the Past Simple and Present Perfect.

Past Simple
1. The Past Simple refers to an action that happened at a definite time in the past.
   He **died** in 1882.
   She **got** married when she was 22.
   The action is finished.
   I **lived** in Bangkok for a year (but not now).
2. Time expressions + the Past Simple

	in 1999.
	last week.
I did it	two months **ago**.
	on March 22.
	for two years.

Present Perfect
1. The Present Perfect refers to an action that happened at an indefinite time in the past.
   She **has won** awards.
   She**'s written** 20 songs.
   The action can continue to the present.
   She**'s lived** there for 20 years (and she still does.)
2. Time expressions + the Present Perfect

	for 20 years.
I've worked here	**since** 1995.
	since I graduated from school.

   We've **never** been to Costa Rica.

2. Compare these sentences.

✗	I've broken my leg last year.
✓	I broke my leg last year.

✗	He works as a musician all his life.
✓	He has worked as a musician all his life.

✗	When have you been to Mexico?
✓	When did you go to Mexico?

✗	How long do you have your car?
✓	How long have you had your car?

Unit 8

8.1 *have to/have got to*

Form

has/have + *to* + infinitive

Affirmative and negative

I We You They	have don't have		
		to	work hard.
He She It	has doesn't have		

Question

Do	I we you they		
		have to	work hard?
Does	he she it		

Short answer

Do you have to wear a uniform?	Yes, I do.
Does he have to go now?	No, he doesn't.

Note

The past tense of *have to* is *had to*, with *did* and *didn't* in the question and the negative.

> I **had to** get up early this morning.
> Why **did** you **have to** work last weekend?
> They liked the hotel because they **didn't have to** do any cooking.

Use

1. *Have to* expresses a general obligation. The obligation comes from "outside"—perhaps a law, a rule at school or work, or someone in authority.
   > You **have to** have a driver's license if you want to drive a car. (That's the law.)
   > I **have to** start work at 8:00. (My company says I must.)
2. *Have got to* can be used to express a specific obligation. This is something that must be done "right now."
   > It's 10:00. I**'ve got to** leave.
3. *Don't/doesn't have to* expresses absence of obligation (it isn't necessary).
   > You **don't have to** wash the dishes. I have a dishwasher.
   > She **doesn't have to** work on Monday. It's her day off.

8.2 Introduction to modal auxiliary verbs

Form

These are modal auxiliary verbs.

can could might must should will would

They are looked at in different units of Headway.

They have certain things in common:
1. They "help" another verb. The verb form is the infinitive without *to*.
   > She **can** drive.
   > I **must get** my hair cut.

2. There is no *do/does* in the question.
   > **Can she sing**?
   > **Should I go** home now?
3. The form is the same for all persons. There is no *-s* in the third person singular:
   > He **can dance** very well.
   > She **should try** harder.
   > It **will rain** soon.
4. To form the negative, add *n't*. There is no *don't/doesn't*.
   > I wouldn**'t** like to be a teacher.
   > You must**n't** steal.

   #### Note
   will not = won't.
   > It **won't** rain tomorrow.
5. Most modal verbs refer to the present and future.
   Only *can* has a past tense form, *could*.
   > I **could** swim when I was three.

8.3 *should*

Form

should + infinitive without *to*
The forms of *should* are the same for all persons.

Affirmative and negative

I He We They	should do more exercise. shouldn't tell lies.

Question

Should	I she they	see a doctor?	
Do you think	I he we	should see a doctor?	

Short answer

Should I phone home?	Yes, you should.
Should I buy a motorcycle?	No, you shouldn't.

Use

Should is used to express what the speaker thinks is right or the best thing to do. It expresses mild obligation or advice.

> I **should** do more work. (This is my opinion.)
> You **should** do more work. (I'm telling you what I think.)
> Do you think we **should** stop here? (I'm asking you for your opinion.)

Shouldn't expresses negative advice.

> You **shouldn't** sit so close to the TV. It's bad for your eyes.

Note

Should expresses the opinion of the speaker, and it is often introduced by *I think* or *I don't think*.

> **I think** politicians **should** listen more.
> **I don't think** people **should** get married until they're 21.

8.4 *must*

Form

must + infinitive without *to*
The forms of *must* are the same for all persons.

Affirmative and negative

I He We They	must try harder. mustn't steal.

Questions with *must* are possible, but the use of *have to* is more common.

Question	Short answer
Must I take tests? Do I **have to** take tests?	Yes, you must. Yes, you do.

Use

1. *Must* expresses strong obligation. Generally, this obligation comes from "inside" the speaker.
   I **must** get my hair cut. (I think this is necessary.)
2. Because *must* expresses the authority of the speaker, you should be careful of using *You must* … . It sounds very bossy!
   You **must** help me. (I am giving you an order.)
   Could you help me? is much better.
3. *You must* … can express a strong suggestion.
   You must see the Monet exhibition. It's wonderful.
   You must give me a call when you're in town again.

Unit 9

9.1 Time clauses

1. Look at this sentence.
   I'll give her a call when I get home.
   It consists of two clauses: a main clause *I'll give her a call* and a secondary clause *when I get home.*
2. These conjunctions of time introduce secondary clauses.

when	while	as soon as	after	before	until

   They are not usually followed by a future form. They refer to future time, but we use a present tense.
   When I get home, I'll …
   While we're away, …
   As soon as I hear from you, …
   Wait here **until** I get back.

9.2 *will*

Form

For the forms of *will*, see p. 144.

Use

1. *Will* expresses a decision or intention made at the moment of speaking.
   Give me your case. **I'll** carry it for you.
2. It also expresses a future fact. The speaker thinks "This action is sure to happen in the future."
   Boston **will** win the game.
   Tomorrow's weather **will** be warm and sunny.
   This use is like a neutral future tense. The speaker is predicting the future, without expressing an intention, plan, or personal judgement.

9.3 First conditional

Form

if + Present Simple, *will* + infinitive without *to*

Affirmative and negative

If	I work hard, I she has enough money, she we don't hurry up, we you're late, I	'll (will) won't	pass the test. buy a new car. be late. wait for you.

Question

What Where	will	you do she go	if	you don't go to college? she can't find a job?

Short answer

Will you go to college if you graduate? If we look after the planet, will we survive?	Yes, I will. No, I won't. Yes, we will. No, we won't.

Note

The condition clause *if* … can come at the beginning of the sentence or at the end. If it comes at the beginning, we put a comma at the end of the clause. If it comes at the end, we do not use a comma.
   If I work hard, I'll pass the exam.
   I'll pass the exam **if** I work hard.

Use

The first conditional is used to express a possible condition and a probable result in the future.
   If my check **comes**, **I'll buy** us all dinner.
   You**'ll get** wet if you **don't take** an umbrella.
   What**'ll happen** to the environment if we **don't look after** it?

Note

1. English uses a present tense in the condition clause, not a future form.
   If it **rains** …   NOT   If it ~~will rain~~ …
   If I **work** hard …   NOT   If ~~I'll work~~ hard …
2. *If* expresses a possibility that something will happen; *when* expresses what the speaker sees as certain to happen.
   If I find your book, I'll send it to you.
   When I get home, I'll take a bath.

Unit 10

10.1 Verb patterns 2

Verb patterns were first covered in Unit 5. There is a list of verb patterns on p. 153.

1. Verb + *to* + infinitive
   They **managed to escape**.
   I **try to visit** somewhere new.
   We **decided to go** abroad.
2. *go* + *-ing* for sports and activities
   Let's **go skiing**.
   We **went dancing**.
3. Verb + sb + infinitive without *to*
   My teachers **made** me **work** hard.
   My parents **let** me **go out** when I want.

10.2 *used to*

Form

used + *to* + infinitive
Used to is the same in all persons.

Affirmative and negative

I She We They	used to didn't use to	smoke. like cooking.

Question

What did you use to do?

Short answer

Did you use to smoke a lot?	Yes, I did./No, I didn't.

Note

1. The question form is not often used. We ask a question in the Past Simple, and reply using *used to*.
   Where **did** you **go** on vacation when you were young?
   We **used to go** camping in the mountains.
2. *Never* is often used.
   I **never** used to watch TV.
3. Be careful not to confuse to *use* (e.g., *I* **use** *a knife to cut an apple.*) and *used to*.
   The pronunciation is also different.
   to use /yuz/   used to /yustu/ or /yustə/

Use

Used to is used:
1. to express a past habit.
   He **used to** play soccer every Saturday, but now he doesn't.
2. to express a past state.
   They **used to** be happy together, but now they fight all the time.

10.3 *used to* and the Past Simple

1. The Past Simple can also be used to express a past habit or state.
   He **played** soccer every Sunday when he **was** a boy.
   They **were** happy together when they **were** first married.
2. Only the Past Simple can be used for actions which happened once in the past.
   We used to go to Canada every summer, but once, in 1987, we **went** to Mexico.
   Last night I **drank** champagne.

Note

Used to has no equivalent in the present. The Present Simple is used for present habits and states.
   She **lives** in Tokyo.
   She sometimes **comes** to Chicago on business.

10.4 Infinitives

1. Infinitives are used to express purpose. They answer the question *Why* ... ? This use is very common in English.
   I'm learning English **to get** a good job.
   She's saving her money **to buy** a car.
   I'm going to Scotland **to visit** my parents.

Note

Some languages express this idea of purpose with a translation of *for* + infinitive. English does not use *for*.
   I came here **to learn** English.
   NOT   I came here ~~for to~~ learn English.
            I came here ~~for~~ learn English.

2. Infinitives are used after certain adjectives.

I'm	pleased surprised	to see you.
It's	hard important impossible	to learn Chinese.

3. Infinitives are used after the question words *who, what, where, how*, etc.
   Can you tell me **how to get** to the station?
   I don't know **who to speak** to.
   Show me **what to do**.
4. Infinitives are used after the compounds *something, nothing, nowhere, anybody*, etc.
   Have **something to eat**!
   I have **nothing to do**.
   There's **nowhere to hide**.
   Is there **anyone to talk** to?

Unit 11

11.1 The passive

Form

am/is/are was/were has/have been will	+ past participle

The past participle of regular verbs ends in *-ed*. There are many common irregular verbs. See the list on p. 153.

Present

Affirmative and negative

English **is spoken** all over the world.
Toyota cars **are made** in Japan.
My children **aren't helped** with their homework.
Coffee **isn't grown** in England.

Question

Where **is** rice **grown**?
Are cars **made** in your country?

Past

Affirmative and negative

My car **was stolen** last night.
The animals **were frightened** by a loud noise.
He **wasn't injured** in the accident.
The thieves **weren't seen** by anyone.

Question

How **was** the window **broken**?
Were the plants **watered** last night?

Present Perfect

Affirmative and negative

I**'ve been robbed**!
Diet Coke **has been made** since 1982.
They **haven't been invited** to the party.

Question

How many times **have** you **been hurt** playing soccer?
Has my car **been repaired**?

will

Affirmative and negative

Ten thousand cars **will be produced** next year.
The cars **won't be sold** in the United States.

Question

Will the children **be sent** to a new school?

Short answer

Are cars made in your country?	Yes, they are./No, they aren't.
Were the plants watered last night?	Yes, they were./No, they weren't.
Has my car been repaired?	Yes, it has./No, it hasn't.
Will these cars be produced next year?	Yes, they will./No, they won't.

Note

1. The rules for tense usage in the passive are the same as in the active.
   Present Simple to express habit:
   My car **is serviced** regularly.
   Past Simple to express a finished action in the past:
   Television **was invented** by John Logie Baird.
   Present Perfect to express an action which began in the past and continues to the present:
   Diet Coke **has been made** since 1982.
2. The passive infinitive (*to be* + past participle) is used after modal auxiliary verbs and other verbs which are followed by an infinitive.
   Driving should **be banned** in city centers.
   The house is going **to be knocked down**.

Use

1. The object of an active verb becomes the subject of a passive verb. Notice the use of *by* in the passive sentence.

   Object

   Active   Shakespeare wrote Hamlet.

   Passive   Hamlet was written by Shakespeare.

   Subject

2. The passive is not another way of expressing the same sentence in the active. We choose the active or the passive depending on what we are more interested in.
   Hamlet **was written** in 1600. (We are more interested in *Hamlet*.)
   Shakespeare **wrote** comedies, histories, and tragedies. (We are more interested in Shakespeare.)

Note

Some verbs, for example, *give, send, show*, have two objects, a person and a thing.
   She **gave me** a **book** for my birthday.
In the passive, we often make the person the subject, not the thing.
   I was given a book for my birthday.
   She was sent the information by mail.
   You'll be shown where to sit.

Unit 12

12.1 Second conditional

Form

if + Past Simple, *would* + infinitive without *to*
Would is a modal auxiliary verb. There is an introduction to modal auxiliary verbs on p. 147.
The forms of *would* are the same for all persons.

Affirmative and negative

If	I had more money, I she knew the answer, she we lived in China, we I didn't have so many debts, I	'd (would) wouldn't	buy a DVD player. tell us. soon learn Chinese. have to work so hard.

Question

What Which countries	would	you do you go to	if	you had a year off? you traveled around the world?

Short answer

Would you travel around the world? If they had the money, would they buy a new car?	Yes, I would./No, I wouldn't. Yes, they would./No, they wouldn't.

Note

1. The condition clause can come at the beginning or the end of the sentence. If it comes at the beginning, we put a comma at the end of the clause. If it comes at the end, we do not use a comma.
   If I had more time, I'd help.
   I'd help **if** I had more time.
2. *Were* is often used instead of *was* in the condition clause.
   If I **were** you, I'd go to bed.
   If he **were** smarter, he'd know he was making a mistake.

Use

The second conditional is used to express an unreal or improbable condition and its probable result in the present or future.
The condition is unreal because it is different from the facts that we know. We can always say "But … ."
   If I were president, **I'd increase** taxes for rich people. (But I'm not president.)
   If I lived in a big house, **I'd have** a party. (But I live in a small house.)
   What **would** you **do if you saw** a ghost? (But I don't expect that you will see a ghost.)

Note

1. The use of the past tense (*If I had*) and *would* does not refer to past time. Both the first and second conditional refer to the present and the future. The past verb forms are used to show "This is different from reality."
   If I win the tennis game, **I'll be** happy. (I think I have a good chance.)
   If I won a thousand dollars, **I'd …** (But I don't think I will.)
2. We do not use *would* in the condition clause.
   If the weather **was** nice …   NOT If the weather ~~would be~~ nice …
   If I **had** more money …   NOT If I ~~would have~~ more money …

12.2 *might*

Form

might + infinitive without *to*
Might is a modal auxiliary verb. For an introduction to modal auxiliary verbs, see p. 147.
The forms of *might* are the same for all persons.

Affirmative and negative

I He It We	might might not	go to the party. be late. rain tomorrow. go out for dinner tonight.

Question

The inverted question *Might you … ?* is unusual. It is very common to ask a question with *Do you think … + will … ?*

Do you think	you'll get here on time? it'll rain? they'll come to our party?

Short answer

Do you think he'll come? Do you think it'll rain?	He might. It might.

Use

1. *Might* is used to express a future possibility. It contrasts with *will*, which, in the speaker's opinion, expresses a future certainty.
   England **will** win the game.
   (I am sure they will.)
   England **might** win the game.
   (It's possible, but I don't know.)
2. Notice that, in the negative, these sentences express the same idea of possibility.
   It **might not** rain this afternoon.
   I **don't think it'll** rain this afternoon.

Unit 13

13.1 Present Perfect Continuous

Form

has/have + been + -ing (present participle)

Affirmative and negative

I We You They	've (have) haven't	been working.
He She It	's (has) hasn't	

Question

How long	have	I we you they	been working?
	has	he she it	

Short answer

Have you been running?	Yes, I have./No, I haven't.
Has he been shopping?	Yes, he has./No, he hasn't.

Use

The Present Perfect Continuous is used:
1. to express an activity which began in the past and continues to the present.
   We**'ve been waiting** here for hours!
   It**'s been raining** for days.
2. to refer to an activity with a result in the present.
   I'm hot because I**'ve been running**.
   I don't have any money because I**'ve been shopping**.

Note
1. Sometimes there is little or no difference in meaning between the Present Perfect Simple and Continuous.
   How long **have you worked** here?
   How long **have you been working** here?
2. Think of the verbs that have the idea of a long time, for example, *wait, work, learn, travel, play*.
   These verbs can be found in the Present Perfect Continuous.
   I**'ve been playing** tennis since I was a child.
   Think of the verbs that don't have the idea of a long time, for example, *find, start, buy, die, lose, break, stop*. It is unusual to find these verbs in the Present Perfect Continuous.
   I**'ve bought** a new dress.
   My cat **has died**.
   My radio**'s broken**.
3. Verbs that express a state, for example, *like, love, know, have* for possession, are not found in the Present Perfect Continuous.
   We**'ve known** each other for a few weeks.
   NOT   We've ~~been knowing~~ each other for a few weeks.
   How long **have** you had your car?
   NOT   How long have you ~~been having~~ your car?
4. The Present Perfect Simple looks at the completed action. This is why, if the sentence gives a number or a quantity, the Present Perfect Simple is used. The Continuous is not possible.
   I**'ve written** three letters today.
   NOT   I've ~~been writing~~ three letters today.

Unit 14

14.1 Past Perfect

Form

had + -ed (past participle)
The past participle of regular verbs ends in *-ed*. There are many common irregular verbs. See the list on p. 153.

Affirmative and negative

I He/She/It We/You/They	'd (had) hadn't	arrived before 10:00.

Question

Had	I he/she/it we/you/they	left?

Short answer

Yes, he had.
No, they hadn't.

Use

The Past Perfect is used to express an action in the past which happened before another action in the past.

Action 2	Action 1

When I got home, John **had cooked** dinner.

Note
Notice the use of the Past Perfect and the Past Simple in the following sentences.
   When I got home, John **cooked** dinner. (First I got home, then John cooked.)
   When I got home, John **had cooked** dinner. (John cooked dinner before I got home.)

14.2 Reported statements

Form

The usual rule is that the verb form moves "one tense back."

Direct speech	Reported speech
Present	**Past**
"I love you."	He said he loved me.
"I'm going out now."	Ann said she was going out.
Present Perfect	**Past Perfect**
"We've met before."	She said they'd met before.
Past Simple	**Past Perfect**
"We met in 1987."	He said they'd met in 1987.
will	**would**
"I'll fix it for you."	She said that she would fix it for me.
can	**could**
"I can swim."	She said she could swim.

Note
Notice the use of *say/tell*.
Say + (that)
   She **said** (**that**) they were happy together.
Tell + person (that)
   He **told me** (**that**) he loved Mary.